Alice Morse Earle

In Old Narragansett

Romances and Realities

Alice Morse Earle

In Old Narragansett
Romances and Realities

ISBN/EAN: 9783744674348

Printed in Europe, USA, Canada, Australia, Japan

Cover: Foto ©Thomas Meinert / pixelio.de

More available books at **www.hansebooks.com**

IN OLD NARRAGANSETT

IN OLD NARRAGANSETT

ROMANCES AND REALITIES

BY

ALICE MORSE EARLE

CHARLES SCRIBNER'S SONS
NEW YORK, 1898

FOREWORD

Some of these stories of old Narragansett are familiar fireside tales to those who have lived in that picturesque land; some are but vague traditions, others summer dreams; a few are family chronicles; still others are outlined in that interesting memoir, Thomas R. Hazard's "Recollections of the Olden Times," or in Updike's "Narragansett Church." Old Narragansett was, properly, all the lands occupied by the Narragansett Indians at the coming of the English. Narragansett is now, popularly, the coast sweep of the western shore of Narragansett Bay from Wickford to Point Judith. In 1685 Narragansett was made a separate government apart from Rhode Island, and was called the King's Province. When reunited with Rhode Island this was changed to King's County. For many years, and by some old people to-day, it is called the South

County, but its legal name is Washington County, which was given it in 1781 ; Washington being a more agreeable and tolerable name at that date to loyal Americans than King's. Narragansett was owned by a comparatively small number of persons, and estates were large, one family owned a tract nine miles long and three wide. Thomas Stanton had a " lordship " four and a half miles long and two wide. Colonel Champlin owned two thousand acres, Thomas Hazard twelve thousand acres. Farms of five, six, even ten miles square existed.

Thus the conditions of life in colonial Narragansett were widely different from those of other New England colonies. The establishment of and adherence to the Church of England, and the universal prevalence of African slavery, evolved a social life resembling that of the Virginian plantation rather than of the Puritan farm. It was a community of many superstitions, to which the folk-customs of the feast-days of the English Church, the evil communications of witch-seeking Puritan neighbors, the voodooism of the negro slaves, the pow wows of the native red men, all added

*a share and infinite variety. It was a planta-
tion of wealth, of vast flocks and herds, of
productive soil, of great crops, of generous
living; all these are vanished from the life
there to-day, but still the fields are smiling
and the lakes and the bay are blue and
beautiful as of yore; and a second prosperity
is dawning in the old King's Province in
the universal establishment therein of happy
summer-homes.*

*In memory of many perfect days spent on
Narragansett roads and lanes, of days in
Narragansett woods or on the shore, these
pages have been written.*

ALICE MORSE EARLE.

WICKFORD, RHODE ISLAND,
    Midsummer Eve, 1897.

CONTENTS

A NARRAGANSETT ELOPEMENT

A NARRAGANSETT ELOPEMENT

FOUR miles north of Narragansett Pier lies
the old South Ferry, from whence for over
a century ran ferry-boats to a landing on
Conanicut Island. About a mile farther
north there stands on Boston Neck an ancient willow-shaded, gambrel-roofed, weather-beaten house which in the latter part of
the eighteenth century was the scene of a
sadly romantic event. It was built by
Rowland Robinson in the first half of the
century—in 1746—and was originally one
hundred and ten feet long, as the stone
foundations still show. The kitchen and
negro quarters have been demolished, and
the present structure has a front of sixty feet.
The rooms within are models of the simple
style of architecture of that day. The
staircase is specially beautiful with its grace-
fully turned balusters and curious drop
ornaments, and its deep-worn steps of bass-
wood. The walls of all the rooms are wain-

3

scoted in a substantial manner, and the fire-places are ornamented with blue and white Dutch tiles. The heavy timbers and rafters —all cut on the place—have not sagged an inch with the weight of years. Over the fireplace in the dining-room is a panel bearing a smoke-darkened painting which represents a deer-hunt that occurred on the Robinson place while the house was being built. The riders in this picture appear to be standing in their stirrups instead of sitting on their saddles. The great attic in which the slaves are said to have slept contains now a picturesque litter of old sea-chests, spinning-wheels, clock-reels, wool-cards, flax-brakes, yarn-winders, saddles, and pillions; and in the beams of the roof are great iron hooks to which—it is whispered—the slaves of olden times were tied when they received their floggings. They are with much more probability the loom-hooks which were used by weavers when weaving cloth on an old hand-loom. The handsome great west room is known as the Lafayette Chamber, it having been occupied for some weeks by the Marquis de Lafayette during the Revolutionary War; and on panes of glass, still whole after a century's use, are the names of French officers, scratched on with the writers' diamond rings.

The house abounds in cupboards — tall, narrow cupboards high up over the chimney, low, broad cupboards under the window-seats, medicine cupboards and pot cupboards, triangular corner cupboards, and, in the parlor, one beautifully proportioned apse-shaped china-cupboard which is ornamented with carved "sunbursts" and scalloped and serrated shelves, and is closed with glass doors to show the treasures and beauties within. But in "Unfortunate Hannah's" chamber is the most famous cupboard of all, for in that narrow and shallow retreat a beautiful daughter of Rowland Robinson hid her lover when she heard the approaching footsteps of her irascible father on the staircase leading to her room.

Rowland Robinson was a typical Narragansett planter—wealthy, proud, and imperious. Tall and portly, ruddy of face, he showed in his dress and carriage his great wealth and high position. A coat of fine dark cloth or velvet with silver buttons was worn over a long yellow waistcoat with great pockets and flaps; violet or brown velvet knee-breeches with handsome top-boots, or silk stockings with buckled shoes ; lace-frilled shirts ; a great beaver cocked hat looped up with cords over his powdered hair—this attire gave him a comely and elegant presence. His character may be given in a few words by quoting the wife of Hon. William Hunter, minister to Brazil. She wrote in her diary sixty years ago her personal recollection of him. "He was of violent passions, which was characteristic of the Robinsons, but of benevolent, noble nature." Many stories are told of his impetuous generosity and kindly impulsiveness, none being more characteristic than his action when his first cargo of slaves came from the Guinea coast. Slave-dealing was such a universal practice at that date among wealthy residents of Narragansett and Newport that it was a commonplace business enterprise for Rowland Robinson, when he was building his new house, to send a ship to Africa for a cargo of negroes, intending to keep the most promising ones for his own household and farm servants, and to sell the remainder. But when the ship landed at South Ferry, and the forlorn, wretched, feeble men and women disembarked, he burst into tears and vowed that not one should be sold. He kept them all in his own household, where they were always kindly treated. He never again sent a vessel to Africa to engage in the slave-trade, though one negro of royal birth—Queen Abigail—was so happy in her Narragansett home, that with Rowland Robinson's consent and his liberal assistance she returned to her home in Africa, found her son—the negro prince—and brought him to America, where he became Mr. Robinson's faithful body-servant.

The wealthy planter had other sources of income than slave-trading. He owned great ships that engaged in general commerce. He had an immense dairy and made fine Rhode Island cheese from the milk of his beautiful " blanket-cows." It was his ambition to have one hundred of these lovely black-and-white animals, but it is a matter of tradition that, while he could keep ninety-nine readily enough, when he bought or raised the hundredth cow, one of the ninety-nine sickened and died, or was lost through accident, and thus the number still fell short. Great quantities of grain and hay did he also raise on his fertile farm ; and besides the grain and cheese that he shipped to the West Indies he also sold to the wealthy colonists many Narragansett pacers—swift horses of the first distinctively American breed. These pacers all came from one sire, "Old Snip," who it is said was of Andalusian birth and was found swimming in the ocean off the coast of Africa, was hauled on board a trading-ship and was carried to Narragansett, where he was allowed to run wild on the Point Judith tract. These sure-footed pacers had a peculiar gait; they did not sway their rider from side to side, nor jolt him up and down, but permitted him to sit quietly, and thus endure without fatigue a long journey. In those carriageless days, when nearly all travel was by saddle and pillion, the broad-backed, easy-going Narragansett pacers were in such demand that they brought high prices and proved a good source of income.

Three children were born to the builder of this beautiful colonial home: William Robinson, who died in Newport in 1804, in a house on the corner of Broadway and Mann Avenue, and two daughters, Mary and Hannah. Gay festivities had .these young people in the hospitable great house, especially when a demure young Quaker cousin was sent to them to live ⸴for awhile in order to break up a romantic love-affair of hers with a young French officer. Count Rochambeau was a guest at her father's house, and too many opportunities for love-making were found when the young Frenchman came to report to his commanding officer.

Gayest and loveliest of all the beauties throughout Narragansett was fair Hannah Robinson—Unfortunate Hannah. Much testimony of her extraordinary beauty has descended to us, one story being of her meeting with Crazy Harry Babcock, that reckless dare-devil of a soldier whose feats of valor by land and sea were known all over Europe as well as in America. This extraordinary man, during a visit to England, was invited to the palace and introduced to the royal family. When the queen extended her hand to him to be kissed, he sprang briskly from his knees, exclaiming: "May it please your majesty, in my country, when we salute a beautiful woman we kiss her lips, not her hand," and with the words he seized the astonished queen by the shoulders and impressed on her lips a rousing smack. Upon his return to America he

went to Narragansett for the avowed purpose of "seeing the prettiest woman in
Rhode Island." As he entered the parlor
of Rowland Robinson's house fair Hannah
rose to meet him, and the crazy colonel, as
she extended her hand to greet him, dropped
on his knee with a look of intense admira-
tion, saying, in the stilted words of the
times: " Pray permit one who has kissed
unrebuked the lips of the proudest queen on
earth to press for a moment the hand of an
angel from heaven!"

The great wealth and luxurious manner of
living of the opulent Narragansett planters was
shown in no way more plainly than in the
manner in which they educated their children. They spared no pains nor expense to
obtain the best masters and teachers. Rowland Robinson sent his daughter to Newport
to receive instruction from Madame Osborne,
whose fame as a teacher was known throughout America, and whose " Memoirs " form
the dullest book in the English language. At
this school Hannah met the handsome lover
who was to have such an influence over her
life. Pierre Simond, or Peter Simons as was
most unromantically Anglicized his name,
was a scion of a French Huguenot family,

who taught music and French in Madame
Osborne's school. From the moment the
young couple met they were lovers. Both
knew, however, how hopeless it was to think
of obtaining Mr. Robinson's consent to a
marriage which would appear to him so
unequal; they therefore kept their love a
secret.

As the time approached for Hannah's return to her home in Narragansett, the lovers
were in despair at the thought of separation,
for they knew their unhappiness could not
be mitigated even by the exchange of love-
letters. At this juncture the young music-
teacher managed to obtain a position as pri-
vate tutor in the family of Colonel Gardiner,
who lived only two miles from Hannah's
home and who was her uncle.

It can easily be divined that when once in
Narragansett the happy lovers found many
opportunities of meeting, which were frequently brought about by the romantic and
easy-going colonel, and were not hindered
by Hannah's mother when she discovered
her daughter's love-affair. Though Mrs.
Robinson would not give her approval she
tacitly gave her aid by helping to conceal
the lovers' meetings from Rowland Robin-

son ; and it was with her knowledge that the lover came to Hannah's chamber, where he often had to be concealed in the friendly cupboard.

When Peter Simons could not enter the Robinson house he stood by his true-love's window under a great lilac-bush, which is still growing, sturdy and unbroken under the weight of a century of years. In the concealing shadow of the lilac-bush words of love might be whispered to the fair girl who leaned from the window, or letters might be exchanged with comparative safety.

But true love ran no smoother in the eighteenth century than in the nineteenth, and when one night a fair hand dropped a tender billet into the gloom of the lilac-bush, old Rowland Robinson chanced to open the door of his house and he saw the white messenger descend. Speechless with suspicion and rage he rushed to the lilac-bush and thrust his buckthorn stick into it with vigorous blows until a man ran out into the darkness, whom the irate father in the second's glimpse recognized as the "wretched French dancing-master" who taught his nephews.

The horrified and disgusted anger of Rowland Robinson and the scene that ensued

within doors can well be imagined; little
peace or happiness was there for Hannah
after her father's discovery. Updike, in his
" History of the Narragansett Church," says
of her life at this time: " If she walked,
her movements were watched; if she rode,
a servant was ordered to be in constant at-
tendance; if a visit was contemplated, her
father immediately suspected it was only a
pretext for an arranged interview; and even
after departure, if the most trifling circum-
stance gave color to suspicion, he would immediately pursue and compel her to return.
In one instance she left home to visit her
aunt in New London; her father soon afterward discovered from his windows a vessel leaving Newport and taking a course
toward the same place.   Although the vessel
and the persons on board were wholly unknown to him, his jealousies were immediately aroused.   Conjecturing it was Mr.
Simons intending to fulfil an arrangement
previously made, he hastened to New London, arrived a few hours only after his
daughter, and insisted on her instant return.
No persuasions or argument could induce
him to change his determination, and she
was compelled to return with him."

Though Rowland Robinson was firm in his determination and constant in his action to prevent the lovers from meeting, Hannah —the true daughter of her father—was equally determined not to give up her sweetheart ; and as the Narragansett neighbors, like the rest of the world, "dearly loved a lover," they gladly assisted the romance by exchanging letters and arranging meetings for the lovers. Months of harassing suspicions and angry words at home, and frightened meetings with her lover away from home, told so upon Hannah's health that her mother finally permitted to be carried into execution a long-planned scheme of elopement. It was finally arranged through the agency and assistance of a young friend of Hannah's —Miss Belden—and the ever sentimental colonel-uncle.

Invitations for a great ball had been sent out all over Narragansett, and to many in Boston, Providence, and Newport. It was to be given by Mrs. Updike, Hannah's aunt. She lived eight miles north of Rowland Robinson's home, in the old historic house which is still standing and is now known as Cocumcussuc. A portion of it was the first house or fort built by the English in

Narragansett in the year 1636. Though
Hannah's father was unwilling to allow his
daughter out of his sight, he at last consent-
ed that both Hannah and Mary should go to
their aunt's ball. They set out on horseback, accompanied by faithful Prince, the son
of Queen Abigail, and were met, as had been
arranged, in the thick woods on the top of
Ridge Hill, by Mr. Simons with a closed
carriage. Into this conveyance Hannah entered with her lover, in spite of her sister's
tears and Prince's frantic appeals, and rode
off to Providence, where the eloping couple
were married.

When the news of Hannah's disobedience
came to the knowledge of Rowland Robinson, his rage and disgust knew no bounds.
He forbade his family ever to communicate
with Hannah again ; and knowing well that
she must have been assisted in carrying out
her plans to elope, he offered a large reward
to anyone who would make known to him
the names of the persons who had aided her
escape.

It would seem that the fair bride should
be called Fortunate Hannah, since she managed to evade her father's vigilance and wed
her ardent French lover, but alas ! Peter

Simons, like many another hero of an elopement, did not prove worthy of the great
sacrifice. Disappointed through the im-
placable anger of Rowland Robinson in the
hope of obtaining any of his wealth, the
unprincipled husband soon neglected his
lovely wife and at last deserted her for
days and weeks. Broken-hearted, alone, and
poor, the unfortunate girl began to fail
rapidly in health, and spent many weary,
lonely days in her wretched home in Providence, having for her only companion her
dog Marcus, that had been secretly sent to
her by her mother from her Narragansett
home.

In the meantime her sister, Mary Robinson, had died of consumption; and her mother, worn out by grief, had completely failed
in health. Her father, though outwardly
stern and unforgiving, was evidently exceedingly unhappy at the alarming news of his
daughter's state of health; and at last, of his
own accord, sent to live with her and care
for her the negro maid who had attended
her in her happy girlhood. He also con-
veyed to her the message that she might
come home and would be warmly welcomed,
provided she would reveal to him the names

of those who assisted in her elopement. Her compliance with this condition was, he said, absolutely imperative.

On receiving this message Hannah wrote in answer, with trembling hand, a most affectionate letter, stating firmly that the sentiments of honor which he himself had both taught and transmitted to her forbade her betraying the confidence of those who had aided her and offended him. Mr. Robinson eagerly opened the letter, but his face changed when he read her decision, and he tossed the sheet to her mother with the contemptuous remark, "Then let the foolish thing die where she is!"

As weeks passed the accounts of Hannah's health grew more alarming still, and it was evident that a fierce struggle between love and pride was taking place in the unhappy father's breast; one day he rose suddenly from the dinner-table, jumped upon his horse, and saying to his wife that he should be away from home for a day or two, started on the thirty-five-mile ride to Providence. He remained overnight at the Updike farm and reached his daughter's house in Providence at noon. Without dismounting he rapped on the door with his riding-whip. Full of joy at the sight of her old master and at the thought of the happy reconciliation, the negro maid hastened to the door with the entreaty that the welcome visitor would come at once to the poor invalid's chamber. " Ask your mistress," said Rowland Robinson, " whether she is now ready to comply with her father's request to know the names of her fellow-conspirators, and say that if she is, he will come in, but on no other conditions." Poor Hannah, torn with a thousand emotions, still clung to her decision not to betray her friends, and her father, without another word, rode away to the Updike farm. For several weeks the stubborn and unhappy father, unable to live without news of his sick daughter, rode at intervals of two or three days from Narragansett to Providence, knocked at Hannah's door, asked for her health, and left without another word.

At last, her friends who had helped in her elopement, hearing of her father's firm decision, which barred all reconciliation, insisted upon her revealing to him their names and the true story ; and when Rowland Robinson next rode up to his daughter's door he received the welcome message that she would see him and tell him all. When he entered that barren chamber all thought of discovering her closely guarded secret fled at once from his thoughts as he gazed at the wasted form of the once beautiful girl. He knelt by her bedside and wept aloud in anguish and remorse. As soon as he recovered his composure he at once rode to his home, from whence he despatched to Providence in a fast-sailing sloop four of his strongest and trustiest negro men, and a hand-litter for the sick, which was, at that time of rough roads and few carriages, an indispensable article in every well-appointed Narragansett household. Dusty, travel-stained, and tired, without waiting for a night's rest he at once jumped upon a fresh horse and, attended by Prince, who was mounted and led a horse for Hannah's maid, poor Rowland Robinson started for the last time to ride to his sick daughter's door.

Upon a lovely morning in June, the four strong negroes, bearing the litter upon which lay the sick girl, with her father and faithful Prince riding on either side, slowly wended their way to poor Hannah's early home. Those who know the beauty of sunny Narragansett in early June, when the roads are everywhere overhung with the graceful, sweet - scented blossoms of slender locust-trees, when the roadsides are one luxuriant, blooming garden of lovely wild flowers, and the fields are sweet with rich clover, can feel the strong and painful contrast which the sad figure of the dying girl must have formed to the glowing life around.

When the spot was reached on Ridge Hill where Hannah had seen for the last time her sister Mary, Prince saw that she covered her face with her hands and cried. One other pathetic incident is told by "Shepherd Tom" of the homeward journey. Though on every side lay a glory of spring flowers, poor Hannah, with thoughts that no one can fathom, asked her father to pick for her and lay on her breast a withered sprig of the pale blossom called life-everlasting, which had bloomed and died the year before.

At last the painful journey was ended; of the sad meeting between mother and daughter, and of the sorrowful faces of the faithful servants, it is needless to write in detail.

That night a whip-poor-will—the bird believed throughout Narragansett to be the

harbinger of death—perched on the lilac-
bush under the window of the chamber
where once again slept Unfortunate Hannah; and throughout the long dark hours
sounded gloomily in the father's ears the
sad, ominous cry of " Whip-poor-will!
Whip - poor - will ! " The following day
poor Hannah died.

Again did four strong men bear on their
shoulders the form of the once beautiful girl,
as they passed under the branches of the
sweet-scented lilac to the grave near the old
house where still is shown the head-stone
that marks the last resting-place of Unfortunate Hannah Robinson.

NARRAGANSETT WEAVERS

NARRAGANSETT WEAVERS

DURING the first years of this century there could be found in every English town, village, and hamlet many hand-looms and many weavers who on these looms wove for their neighbors and for small cloth-jobbers strong homespun woollen stuffs, rag-carpets, woollen sheets, cotton and wool bed-spreads, flannels, coarse linen and tow, heavy cotton cloth and fine table and bed linen. These hand-looms lingered in use till about 1840. So universal was then the extinction of hand-weaving through the vast growth of power-loom manufacture and of spinning by steam-spindle, and so sudden and complete the destruction and vanishing of all the old-time implements and machines, that when, ten years ago, under the stimulus of Ruskin's fiery appeal for the revivifying of hand-spinning and hand-weaving, these household arts were again started in Westmoreland, but a single linen-loom could be found for the work.

In the American colonies hand-weaving was also a universal industrial art. In no part of the country has the industry lingered longer than in old Narragansett. In many old New England towns single hand-looms can be found, some in running order, and with owners capable of running them to make rag-carpets. Others are still standing, cob-webbed and dusty, in attic lofts, lean-to chambers, woodsheds, or barns, with no one to set the piece or fill the shuttles. In Narragansett I know a score of old looms in good running order, though, save in one instance, set only for weaving rag-carpets; in many cases the owners, who do not make weaving a trade, will not "start them up" for weaving less than a hundred yards of carpeting. This is a long strip for a room in a cottage or farm-house, so neighbors frequently join together in ordering these carpets, and in company send vast rolls of the filling, which is made of inch-wide strips of cloth of all colors and materials sewed in long strips. Within a few years these old hand-looms have been used for weaving rag-portières made of silk strips.

Weaving was a very respectable occupation. It is told that the regicide Judge

Whalley lived to great old age in Narragansett—one hundred and three years—and
earned his living by weaving. The son of
the Congregational minister at Narragansett,
Dr. Torrey, was a weaver. The province was
full of weavers. Miss Hazard gives the
names of many in her "College Tom."
With all the spinning-jennies for spinning a
vast supply of thread and yarn, there were
no power-looms in Narragansett till 1812.
Hand-looms made up all the yarn and thread
that were produced. The prince of Narragansett weavers was Martin Read. In 1761
he was baptized in St. Paul's Church as
"Martin Read, an adult, the Parish Clerk."
He was a devoted lover of the church and
was sexton for many years. He led the
singing, and it is said that under his leader-
ship the *Venite* was first chanted in America.
During the troubled and rector-less days of
the Revolution, he helped the parish work
along by reading morning-prayers and the
funeral-service for the dead.

He was apprenticed, an orphan, at seven
years of age to a diaper-weaver, and served
till he was of age, with one term only of
schooling ; but he was ambitious and read
eagerly instructive books, especially on weav-

ing and kindred arts. He married the daughter of an Irish weaver, and soon had journeymen and apprentices, whom he taught to sing as they wove; and when they did not sing the men whistled the airs, and with singing and whistling the work speeded.

This singing at the loom was not a peculiarity of Martin Read's. We know the exclamation of Falstaff: "I would I were a weaver, I could sing Psalms and all manner of songs." Nares says weavers were generally good singers, and that as they sat at their work they practised part-singing. Many of the weavers in Queen Elizabeth's day were Flemish Calvinists and therefore given to psalm-singing, hence Falstaff's reference.

One weaver, named James Maxwell, wrote some "Weaver's Meditations" in rhyme in 1756. The frontispiece of his book—his portrait at his loom—is thus inscribed:

"Lo, how 'twixt heaven and earth I swing,
    And whilst the shuttle swiftly flies,
With cheerful heart I work and sing,
    And envy none beneath the skies."

Martin Read reared his family well, and in the Episcopal Church. His son, Rev. Dr.

Read, preached for many years at Christ's
Church in Poughkeepsie. He wove coverlets,
blankets, broadcloth, flannel, worsted, linen,
tow-cloth, and calamanco. This last was
a glossy woollen twilled fabric, sometimes
woven in a pattern in the warp. James Fon-
taine, a Huguenot weaver, says it was made of
a fine double-twisted worsted. It was much
used for the nightgowns and banians worn
by substantial citizens of the day, and for
women's winter-gowns.

Other goods made by Weaver Read were
duroy, durant, and crocus, a coarse tow-
stuff for servants' wear. This word, crocus,
still may be heard in Virginia, and perhaps
elsewhere in the South, where it was more
and longer used than in Narragansett.

Martin Read lived near the old church he
so dearly loved, and a sightly spot it was for
a home. Still standing beside the church
foundation, the site where the church first
stood, is the deserted house in which Martin Read lived and wove and whistled and
sung. On the road near his home lives to-
day the last of the old-time weavers, one who
can weave woollen and linen stuffs. Hand-
weaving is not with him an accidental industrial makeshift, but his every-day occupa-

tion and means of livelihood. He learned to weave from one of Martin Read's apprentices.

His low, weather-beaten house, set in a close-walled garden, is one of the most picturesque in old Narragansett. We entered from a glory of midsummer sunlight into a cool, pale-green light which penetrated the rooms through the heavy shadows of the rugged old cedar-trees that overhung the roof and the ancient lilacs that pressed close to the windows.

There has ever been associated in my mind with the trade of weaving the pale and sickly appearance and bearing of many English mill weavers; and, though ever of country life, this Yankee weaver was no exception to the rule. His skin, of extreme delicacy, was pale, yet suffused at times with that semi-transparent flush which is seldom seen save on those whose life is wholly indoors. His hair and beard were long and white, and had evidently been light-brown before they were white; his bright blue eyes looked pleasantly and intelligently out from the wisps of white hair. His visible attire was a clean, but collarless, white shirt and a pair of blue overalls; his feet were bare. We mounted with him the narrow enclosed staircase to the loom-loft.

There was such a flood of color out of doors, the fields and trees were so green, the tangle of larkspurs in the garden was so blue, the sunbeams so radiant, that the attic seemed but a dull abiding-place for a summer's day; but as the eye grew accustomed to the dimmer light and learned to avoid the piercing arrows of sunshine that burned in through the heart-shaped holes in the shutters and made every mote of wavering dust in their path a point of unbearable glitter, then the attic seemed quiet and peaceful, and its shadows were grateful; and even the bang, bang of the loom when it was started up was not a garish rattle. Heaps of gay woollen yarns lay under the eaves, and a roll or two of rag-carpeting and strips of worn-out bed-coverlets of various patterns were hung on the beams or piled in heaps. There were vast boxes of cotton twine; and many yarn-beams ready wound, and swifts and quilling-wheels and "scarnes," many in number, thrust under the garret eaves. Among the discarded wool-wheels and flax-wheels heaped high in the corner—obsolete before their fellow, the hand-loom—I did not peer deep. Though

neglected, they are jealously treasured, for
"that was grandma's foot - wheel," and
"Aunt Eunice used that wool-wheel sixty-
two year," showed that what seemed to me
useless lumber was haloed with association
and tradition. I have never seen or felt elsewhere any such picture, any such atmosphere
of an industrial life that is forever past, as that
old-time weaving. The dim half-light of the
loom-room and the darker garret beyond;
the ancient chairs that thrust out a broken
arm, and tables that put forth a claw-foot
from the shadows; the low buzzing of hornets that fluttered against the upper skylight
or hung in dull clusters on the window-frame
—hornets so dull, so feeble, so innocuous in
their helplessness that they seemed the an-
cients of their day; the eerie clamor of swal-
lows in the chimney; the pungent aroma of
"dry, forgotten herbs," that swayed in the
summer wind from every rafter; and the
weaver, pale and silent, laboriously weaving
his slow-growing web with a patience of past
ages of workers, a patience so foreign to our
present high-pressure and double-speed rates
that he seemed a century old, the very spirit
of colonial, nay, of mediæval days.

There was a monotonous yet well-controlled

precision in this weaver's work that was
most soothing, and that seems to be a characteristic influence of the homespun industries. It was felt by Wordsworth and voiced
in his sonnet :

" Grief, thou hast lost an ever-ready friend
   Now that the cottage spinning-wheel is mute."

This precision in work is that of the
skilled hand and thinking brain controlling
the machine, not the vast power of steam re-
lentlessly crowding the overworked body
and dulled brain.

By this hand-weaving, as if to prove Ruskin's glowing and inspiring assertions, this
weaver earns an independent living in intel-
ligent work, of reasonable hours, in a comfortable house, and in conditions favorable
to health—a vast contrast to the overworked,
unhealthy, poorly fed, stultified factory-
worker. His business has so prospered of
late that he has had a trade-card printed at
the village printer's like any other independent manufacturer. From it I learn that he
weaves rag-carpets, bed-coverlets, and hap-
harlots. Hap-harlots, forsooth ! could anyone believe that obsolete word had been

used since Holinshed's day? He wrote in
1570, in his "Chronicles of England,"
etc. :

"Our fathers have lien full oft upon straw pallets
or rough mats, covered onlie with a sheet under coverlets made of dagswain or hap-harlots, and a good
round log under their heads instead of a bolster."

Yet here have been Narragansett weavers
weaving hap-harlots, and sleeping under hap-
harlots, and speaking of hap-harlots as though
three centuries ago were as yesterday. I
presume they have made dagswains also,
since there still exists bills of Narragansett
shepherds for dagging sheep.

The old-time cotton and wool bed-spreads
or coverlets, seen of old on every four-post
bedstead, he now sells for portières and bath-
room rugs, as well as for bed and couch
spreads. They are woven in simple geo-
metric patterns, just as in the times of the
ancient Britons, when the wools of the weft
were dyed with woad and broom. The patterns are nearly all over a century old. He
has a worn pattern-book with bewildering
rules for setting the heddles for over fifty
designs. Quaint of name are the patterns:

"chariot-wheels and church-windows," is a bold, large design; "church-steps," a simpler one; "bachelors' fancy," "devil's fancy," "five doves in a row," "shooting-star," "rising sun," "rail fence," "green veils," offer little in their designs to give reason for their names. "Whig rose," "Perry's Victory," and "Lady Washington's fancy," show an historical influence in naming. "Orange-peel" is simply a series of oblong hexagons honeycombed together. "All summer and all winter" was similar. "Bricks and blocks" is evenly checkered. "Capus diaper" is more a complicated design for weaving damask linen, taking five harnesses. Floral names are common, such as "Dutch tulip," "rose in bloom," "pansies in the wilderness," "five snow-balls," etc.

The loom on which this Narragansett weaver works might be six centuries old. You may see precisely similar ones pictured by Hogarth in the middle of the eighteenth century; and an older one still in the Campanile at Florence, by Giotto, in 1334.

These excerpts from a letter of Weaver Rose's give some pleasant weaver's lore, and are in the lucid, simple, and quaint English to be expected of a man who still weaves and talks of hap-harlots :

"My grandfather and grandmother Robert and Mary Northrup lived at what is now called Stuart Vale but then known as the Fish Pond, in a little hamlet of four houses, only one of which, my grandfather's, is now standing. He owned a shore and fished in the spring and wove some at home and went out amongst the larger farmers working at his trade of weaving, whilst his wife carried on the weaving at home and had a number of apprentices. He learned his trade of weaving of Martin Read, the deacon of St. Paul's Church, who lived a few rods from the church. He died in 1822, his wife lived till 1848. The spool I gave you was made by Langworthy Pierce, a veteran of the Revolution. It has the initials of his name. I send you now one of his shuttles used for weaving broadcloth, and a square of linen I have woven for you of a pattern of five harnesses called Browbey. The looms here in Narragansett were all made by local carpenters. Stephen Northrup made looms, and Freeborn Church made looms and spinning wheels. I have 2 of his make. Friend Earle! more money can be made by weaving than farming. I have wove 30 yards of rag carpet in one day at 10 cents a yard; or 23 cents a yard when I found the warp. There was a man here by the name of Eber Sherman, he called himself Slippery Eber. He died in the war of 1812; his widow worked at spinning for 25 cents per day and supported herself and one son well on that wage. One dollar and a half per week was regular wage for a woman's

work. It took a woman one week to weave a coverlet of 3 yards long and 2½ yards wide. Mahala Doug-
las went out to work at one dollar and a half per week
making butter and cheese, milking seven cows every
week day and nine on Sunday. She died leaving a
large Estate, several thousand dollars, which her
Legatees had no trouble in spending in six weeks.
My grandfather was one of eight children. One
brother was Rev. William Northrup; Thurston
Northrup, another brother, was a school-teacher and
a weaver of coverlets and cloth. John Northrup
was called Weaver John. He was a coverlet weaver.
John Congdon was a maker of Weavers' reeds or
slays. I have 70 or 80 of his make in my house.
I have a reed that my grandfather Northrup had
made when he went to the Island of Rhode Isl-
and weaving Broadcloth. He received 50 cents
per day pay. Good Cream Cheese was 3 cents a
pound at the same time of the Embargo in the war of
1812. I have an Eight and Twenty slay with 29
Beer that cost one dollar, made by John Congdon 70
years ago, as good as when made. He lived in
North Kingston."

The word slay or sley, meaning a weavers'
reed, has not been used commonly in England for many years, and is contemporary
with hap-harlot. A beer was a counting-off
of forty warp-threads.

It may be seen by this letter how many
classes of workmen were kept busily em-
ployed by these homespun industries; mak-

ers of looms, wheels, reeds, scarnes, rad-
dles, temples, swifts, niddy-noddys, spools,
and shuttles; and turners of warp - beams
and cloth-beams. The proper shaping of a
shuttle was as important as the shaping of
a boat's hull. When the shuttle was carefully
whittled out, smoothed off with glass, lightly shod with steel, and marked by burnt-in
letters with the maker's initials, it was a
proper piece of work, one for a craftsman
to be distinctly proud of. Spools could
be turned on a lathe but were marked by
hand. No wonder our weaver loved his old
worn-out rubbish; every piece had been
made and used by his kinsfolk and neighbors, who had put into every spool, shuttle,
and loom good, faithful hand-work ; and, like
the cloths he wove, they wore well.

Weaver Rose would be an unimpeachable
candidate for many of our modern patriotic-
hereditary societies. One great-great-grandfather held a commission under King George
III., which the weaver still has. Others
were members of the provincial assemblies.
Two great-uncles were taken on board a
Yankee privateer in the Revolution, carried
to England to Dartmoor Prison, and never
heard of afterward. The son of one of

those patriots was captured in the War of
1812, and kept eight years at Dartmoor, while
he was mourned in Narragansett as dead.
He was then released, returned home, and
held to his death an office under the government at Wickford, a Narragansett seaport.
One great-uncle was starved to death in the
prison-ship *Jersey* in the Revolution, and
another lost his life in Newport during imprisonment by the British. Grandfather
James Rose was with the famous Kingston
Reds in the Battle of Rhode Island and
other Revolutionary encounters; and the
weaver's father, William Rose, fought in the
War of 1812. His great-great-grandfather
Eldred killed the famous Indian warrior
Hunewell, after that cruel Narragansett
tragedy, the Swamp Fight. Hunewell was
naked and covered with grease, but he was
not slippery enough to escape the bitter
Englishman, who had been fighting for days.
This tragedy was at Silver Spring, about two
miles from the weaver's home. Another
Indian chased Eldred, but without capturing
him. The chase was long, and Eldred did
not spend much time in looking backward,
but he never forgot the Indian's face; and
some years later he met in Newport an Ind-

ian who was very smooth and friendly, but whom he at once recognized as his old-time enemy. The weaver thus grimly and laconically tells the sequel: " Grandfather got an awl and settled it in his forehead and finished him." Great-grandmother Austin was one of sixteen children. Their names were Parvis, Picus, Piersus, Prisemus, Polybius, Lois, Lettice, Avis, Anstice, Eunice, Mary, John, Elizabeth, Ruth, Freelove. All lived to be three-score and ten, and one to be five-score and two years old.

I have dwelt somewhat at length on the sturdy fighting ancestry of this weaver, with a distinct sense of pleasure at the quality of his forebears. He is, in the best sense, a pure American, with not a drop of admixture of the blood from recent immigrations. Some of his ancestors were those who made the original Petaquamscut purchase from the Indians, and here he lives on the very land they purchased. It is such examples as this that give dignity to New England rural life, give us a sense of not being offensively new. In my genealogical researches in England I have not found such cases nearly as common as in New England. Surprise and even annoyance is shown in England at

your expectation and hope to find descend-
ants of the original owners occupying farm-
houses and manors two hundred years old.

Had the weaving been the only portion of
the work done in the farm-house it would
seem an important addition to the round of
domestic duties, but every step in the pro-
duction of clothing was done at home, as ex-
pressed by Miss Hazard of her great-grand-
father's household in Narragansett: "From
the shepherd who dagged the sheep, the
wool-comber who combed the wool, the
spinners who spun, the weavers who wove,
all in regular order till the travelling tailor
made the clothes up, and Thomas Hazard
went to meeting in a suit made from wool of
his own growing." The "all-wool goods,
yard wide," which we so glibly purchase
to-day meant to the Narragansett dame the
work of months from the time the fleeces
were given to her deft fingers. After dag-
locks, bands, feltings, tarred locks, were
skilfully cut out, the white locks were carefully tossed and separated, and tied in net
bags with tallies, to be dyed. The homely
saying, "dyed in the wool," indicated a
process of much skill. Indigo furnished the
blue shades, madder and logwood the red.

Sassafras, fustic, hickory, and oak bark furnished yellow and brown. It will be noted that the old-time dyes were all vegetable. After the dyeing mixed colors could be made by spreading in layers and carding them over and over again. In carding 'wool, the cards should be kept warm and the wool very slightly greased with rape-oil or "swines'-grease." At last the wool was carded into light rolls and was ready for the wheel.

An old writer says, "The action of spinning must be learned by practice, not by relation." The grace and beauty of wool-spinning, ever sung by the poets, need not be described. Stepping lightly backward and forward, with arms at times high in the air, now low at the side, often by the light only of the fire, the worker, no matter what her age, seemed the perfection of the grace of motion ; and the beauty of the occupation makes the name of spinster (the only title by law of every single woman) a title of honor and dignity.

The preparation of flax was infinitely more tedious and more complicated. From the time the tender plant springs up, through pulling, spreading, drying, rippling, stacking, rotting, cleaning, braking, swingling, beetling, ruffling, hetchelling, spreading, and drawing, there are in all over twenty dexterous manipulations till the flax is ready for the wheel, the most skilful manipulation of all, and is wrapped round the spindle. Flax thread was spun on the small flax-wheel. "Lint on the wee wheel, woo' on the muckle." It was reeled into skeins on a clock-reel, which ticked when the requisite number had been wound, when the spinner stopped and tied the skein. A quaint old ballad has the refrain :

"And he kissed Mistress Polly when the clock-reel
    ticked."

These knots of linen thread had to be bleached before they were woven. They were soaked in water for days, and constantly wrung out; they were washed again and again in the brook; they were "bucked" with ashes and hot water in a bucking-tub; they were seethed, soaked, rinsed, dried, and wound on bobbins and quills for the loom. In spite of all this bleaching, the linen web, when woven, would not be white, and it afterward went through twoscore more processes of bucking, possing, rinsing, dry-

ing, and grassing.   In all, forty bleaching
manipulations were necessary for "light
linens."   Thus, at least, sixteen months had
passed since the flax-seed had been sown,
during which the good-wife had not "eaten
the bread of idleness."

With the passing of these old-time household arts of spinning and weaving, went also
the household independence.   Well timed
was our struggle for freedom from British
rule, when every man and wife on their own
farm held everything necessary for life and
comfort—food, shelter, fuel, illumination,
clothing.   What need had he or she to fear
any king?   It could not be such an independent revolt to-day;   in the matter of
clothing alone, no family could be independent of outside assistance.

The old-time preparatory work of the
weaver is much simplified for this Narragansett weaver in modern times, by the use of
machine-spun threads and yarns.   The warp
of these bed coverlets is of strong twine or
thread, while the weft is of various woollen
yarns or zephyrs or crewels, bought at mills.
These latter are aniline-dyed, and in no ar-
tistic sense equal the old indigo, hickory,
sassafras, or madder home-dyed wools of

yore. These skeins of yarn are prepared for use by spreading them on a reel or swifts, and winding the yarn off on quills in a quilling-wheel, which is somewhat like a simplified spinning-wheel.

Besides these weavers who worked in their own homes, making their own wool into cloth to sell, or weaving the thread and yarn brought to them by their neighbors, there was a distinct class of travelling weavers, who went from house to house working for a few shillings a day and their "keep." They often were quaint and curious characters; frequently what were known as "natural preachers;" that is, either mystic or fanatic souls who tried to supplement or supersede the religious teaching of the community by itinerant preaching. Such teachers and preachers have ever flourished in Narragansett since the day of Samuel Gorton and his associates.

One of these weaver-preachers, undismayed by the indifference and even the disapproval of his neighbors, built a rude log pulpit in the woods near his home and there communed aloud with God if not with man. The sound of his fervid prayers and invocations could be heard afar off by passers-by in the wood-lanes and roads, even in mid-winter; while the emphasizing thumps of his sturdy fist kept his blood as warm as his religion and startled the Narragansett squirrels and chipmunks who thriftily used the recesses of the weaver's pulpit as a storage-place for nuts and acorns. There were few women weavers among them, especially for linen-weaving, which was hard work. Occasionally some sturdy woman, of masculine muscle and endurance, was a weaver.

One of these Narragansett women-weavers was a witch. She would sit for hours bending over her loom, silent, peering into it and not doing a single row. This angered the dames for whom she worked, but they said nothing, lest they get her ill-will. Suddenly she would sit up and start her treadle; bang! bang! would go her batten as fast as corn in a corn-popper; and at night, after she had gone home, when her piece was still set in the loom, the family would waken and hear the half-toned clapping of the loom, which someone was running softly to help the witch out in her stint, probably the old black man. So, behold! at the end of the week more cloth appeared on the cloth-beam, more linen was ready for bleaching, and more rolls of carpet were woven than could be turned out by any man-weaver in the province. So whether it was hitching up with the devil or not, she always had employment in plenty; and her fine linen table-cloths were in every bridal outfit, and her linen web used in many a shroud throughout Narragansett.

She never ate with the family of her employer as did every other worker in house or on farm, nor was it evident that she brought food with her. The minister suspected she ate nocake, which she could easily hide in her pockets. She never asked for water, nor cider, nor switchel, nor kill-devil, nor had anyone ever seen her drink. Debby Nichols once saw a bumble-bee fly buzz-buzz out of her mouth as she wove in the minister's loom-loft. But the minister said it was only a hornet flying past her—the garret was full of them. But, sure enough, at that very hour Joe Spink fell from his horse on the old Pequot trail from Wickford and broke his leg. Joe said a big bumble-bee stung the horse on the nose and made him rear and plunge. Joe had had high words with the witch over some metheglin he had tried to buy from her the previous week, for she brewed as well as she wove. The minister said that if metheglin had been the only drink Joe ever bought he wouldn't have fallen from his horse, and that it wasn't the first bee Joe had had in his bonnet.

One day some careless darkies in a kitchen set on fire a hank of tow that was being hetchelled by the chimney-side. The sudden blaze extended to a row of freshly ironed sheets, then to a wool-wheel, and soon a dense smoke and darting flames filled the room. All ran out of the house, some for water, some for buckets, some for help, and no one thought of the witch in the loom-loft. The bang and rattle of her work made her ignorant of the noise and commotion below, and as the smoke entered the loft she thought, " But that chimney do smoke ! " Finally a conviction of danger came to her and she made her way down the loft-ladder and through the entry with difficulty to the open air.

" Where's the cat? " was her abrupt greeting to the shamefaced folk who began to apologize spasmodically for their neglect to alarm her. " I saw her an hour ago on the spare bed in the fore room "—and back into the house rushed the witch, to return

in a few moments with Tabby safely in her
arms. This act of course deserved scant
praise. Everyone murmured that there was
probably some good reason for doing it,
that everyone knew witches and cats had
close relations, that the house didn't burn
down anyway, and probably she knew it
wasn't going to.

One night a neighbor met her, breathing
heavily, her hand at her side, hobbling halt-
ingly homeward. He told his wife he
guessed the witch was pretty sick. She told
the minister's wife that the witch was get-
ting her deserts. The latter in turn told
her husband, and during a ministerial visit
the next day he discoursed profitably on the
probable illness and the unsanctified life of
that misguided woman. The minister sat
long in the front room sipping sangaree, but
the hard-working little tailoress in the kitchen
overheard his moralizing and his story. And
when goose and shears were laid aside, and
her day's work was over, she hurried through
the winter gloaming, across the ice-crusts
of three fields, to the witch's door. No
light shone from the window, either of evil
or domestic significance ; but the tailoress
pulled the latch-string and pushed open the

door, and by the light of her hand-lantern found the witch in the chilled house cold and dead.

The following August a band of wondering, marauding boys, with alternate hesitation and bravado, entered the tenantless house. The windows had all been broken by missiles thrown by witch-hating passersby, and the spring rains and summer suns had freely entered the room. And lo ! the witches bed, on which she died—a sack full of straw of mouse-barley, with occasional spikes of grain attached—had sprouted and grown through the coarse hempen bed-tick, and was as green and flourishing as the grass over her unmarked grave.

WHERE THREE TOWNS MEET

WHERE THREE TOWNS MEET

In the heart of Narragansett three towns meet at a cross-roads ; they are North Kingston, South Kingston, and Exeter.   It is a lonely cross-roads, even in days of summer, though Weaver Rose's cheerful home is near it ; but it is picturesque and beautiful in its extended view, its overreach of splendid locust-trees, and the tangle of wild flowers fringing the roadside and rioting along the stone walls.   There is no monument or stone, nothing to mark the special tradition of this corner, as Squaw Rock at Indian Corner, half a mile farther on the road, a sinister rock with dark, blood-red veins and splashes, a rock whereon were dashed the brains of a Narragansett squaw by her drunken brave of a husband.

This cross-roads, or " corner," has been the scene many times of episodes as uncivilized, if not as cruel, as the one that immortalized Squaw Rock.   Here—a spot chosen either through fancy, tradition, or even rustic fashion, or because here three townships meet—have taken place several of those absurd bequests of barbaric peoples known as shift-marriages.

These ungallant and extremely inconvenient ceremonies are not American inventions or Yankee notions, but an old English custom, being in brief the marriage of a woman, usually a widow, clad only in her shift, to avoid hampering her newly made husband with her old debts. All through New England, in New York and Pennsylvania, this custom was known until this century. In Narragansett it was comparatively common. The exact form of the *sacrifice* (for sacrifice it was of modesty to the new husband's cupidity) and notions about it varied in localities. Let me give a marriage-certificate of a shift-marriage which took place on this very cross-roads where the three towns meet:

"On March 11th, 1717, did Philip Shearman Take the Widow Hannah Clarke in her Shift, without any other Apparel, and led her across the Highway, as the Law directs in such Cases and was then married according to law by me. WILLIAM HALL, *Justice.*"

It is not specified in this certificate that this grotesque proceeding took place at night,

but, out of some regard for decency, and to
avoid notoriety, such was usually the case.

There is an ancient registration book of
births, deaths, and marriages at the handsome
new Town Hall at South Kingston, R. I.
There is an entry within it of a shift-marriage :

"Thomas Calverwell was joyned in marriage to
Abigail Calverwell his wife the 22. February, 1719–
20. He took her in marriage after she had gone four
times across the highway in only her shift and hair-
lace and no other clothing. Joyned together in
marriage by me.

"GEORGE HAZARD, *Justice.*"

This was but two years after the marriage
of Widow Clarke, and the public parade
may have taken place on the same spot, but
there is a slight variation, in that the fair
Abigail's ordeal was prolonged to four times
crossing the road. The naming of the hair-
lace seems trivial and superfluous with such
other complete disrobing, but it was more
significant than may appear to a careless
reader. At that date women wore caps even
in early girlhood, and were never seen in
public without them. To be capless indicated complete dishabille. A court record
still exists wherein is an entry of a great in-

sult offered to the town constables by an angry and contemptuous woman. She threatened to pull off her head-gear and go before them, " only in her hair-lace and hair, like a parcel of pitiful, beggarly curs that they were." So the abandon of only a hairlace comported well with Abigail Calverwell's only a shift.

Hopkinton is another Narragansett town, in the same county. In 1780 David Lewis married at Hopkinton, Widow Jemima Hill, " where four roads meet," at midnight, she being dressed only in her shift. This was to avoid payment of Husband Hill's debts. Ten years later, in a neighboring town, Richmond, still in the South County, Widow Sarah Collins appeared in the twilight in a long shift, a special wedding-shift covering her to her feet, and was then and thus married to Thomas Kenyon.

Westerly, still in the same Narragansett county, had the same custom and the same belief.

" To all People whom It May Concern. This Certifies that Nathanell Bundy of Westerly took ye Widdow Mary Parmenter of sd town on ye highway with no other clothing but shifting or smock on ye Evening of ye 20 day of Aprill, 1724, and was joined

together in that honorable Estate of matrimony in ye
presence of   JOHN SANDERS, *Justice.*
  " JOHN COREY.
  " GEORGE COREY.
  " MARY HILL.
  " PETER CRANDALL.
  " MARY CRANDALL."

The use of the word smock here recalls the
fact that in England these marriages were
always called smock-marriages.

The Swedish traveller, Kalm, writing in
1748, tells of one Pennsylvania bridegroom
who saved appearances by meeting the scan-
tily clad widow half-way from her house to
his own, and announcing formally that the
wedding-garments which he thereupon pre-
sented to her were not given to her but were
only lent to her for this occasion.   This is
much like the ancient custom of marriage in-
vestiture, still in existence in Eastern Hin-
dostan.

Another husband who thus formally lent
wedding-garments to a widow-bride was
Major Moses Joy, who married Widow Hannah Ward in Newfane, Vt., in 1789.   The
widow stood in her shift, within a closet, and
held out her hand through a diamond-shaped
hole in the door to the Major, who had gal-

lantly deposited the garments for Madam to don before appearing as a bride. In Vermont many similar marriages are recorded, the bride not being required to cross the highway. One of these unclad brides left the room by a window, and dressed on the upper rounds of a ladder, a somewhat difficult feat even for a "lightning-change artist." In Maine the custom also prevailed. One half-frozen bride, on a winter's night in February, was saved for a long and happy life by having the pitying minister, who was about to marry her, throw a coat over her as she stood in her shift on the king's highway. In early New York, in Holland, in ancient Rhynland, this avoidance of debt-paying was accomplished in less annoying fashion by a widow's appearing in borrowed clothing at her husband's funeral, or laying a straw or key on the coffin and kicking it off.

The traveller, Gustavus Vasa, records a shift marriage which he saw in New York in 1784. A woman, clad only in her shift, appeared at the gallows just as an execution was about to take place, demanded the life of the criminal, and was then and there married to him. It is well known that in England criminals sentenced to death (usu-

ally for political offences) were rescued from
the gallows by the appearance at the time
and place of execution of women who
claimed the right of marrying them, and
thus saving their lives.

It has been asserted that these shift-marriages were but an ignorant folk-custom, and
that there never was any law or reason for
the belief that the observance procured im-
munity from payment of past debts. But it
is plainly stated in many of these Narragansett certificates that it was " according to the
law in such cases." The marriages were
certainly degrading in character, and were
gone through with only for the express purpose of debt evasion, and they must have
been successful. The chief actors in these
Narragansett comedies were, from scant negative testimony of their life and the social
position of their families, not necessarily of
limited means. Any man of wealth might
not, however, wish to pay the debts of his
matrimonial " predecessor," as the first husband is termed in one case.

And it should be remembered also that at
the time these weddings took place there was
nothing boorish in the community. Con-
sidering the necessary differences in the cen-

turies, the "South County" was not nearly as "countrified," to use a conventional term, then as now. Exeter has ever been sparsely settled, with many woodlands, meagre farms, and little wealth, though it had one church with a thousand members; but North Kingston had a thrifty and enterprising general population, with many men of wealth, and handsome houses. South Kingston, the nearest town-centre to the cross-roads, was settled by men of opulence and of polite culture. It was the richest town in the State of Rhode Island, paying, as late as 1780, double the taxes assigned to Newport and one-third more than Providence. The cross-roads, where the three towns meet, was not far from St. Paul's Church, where the planters and their families gathered each Sunday, riding to it over the very highway where the shift-marriages took place.

As I sat on a fallen tree last summer at the lonely cross-roads, the scene of so many of these shift-marriages, the place, with its fairly tropical bloom, seemed a romantic spot for such a grotesquery; but the picture of the last of these benumbed brides, who, early in this century, clad only in a linen shift, on a February night—a *New England Febru-*

ary night—shivered across the frozen road to avoid the payment of some paltry debt, and the thought of the unspeakable husband who would let her go through such a mortifying and distressing ordeal, there seemed scant romance, and nothing but ignorant and sordid superstition.

TUGGIE BANNOCKS'S MOONACK

TUGGIE BANNOCKS'S MOONACK

TUGGIE BANNOCKS, the Narragansett negress, decided to work a charm on old Bosum
Sidet, the negro tinker. She was not going
to charm him in the ordinary commonplace
way, albeit pleasing, that most dames follow
—be they old or young, black or white—to
allure human beings of the opposite sex.
Her charm was, alas, a malignant one, a
"conjure," that she angrily decided to work
upon him as a revenge for his clumsy and
needless destruction of her best copper tea-
kettle while he was attempting, or I suspect
pretending, to repair it. This charm was not
a matter of a moment's hasty decision and
careless action ; it required some minute and
varied preparation and considerable skill to
carry it out successfully, and work due and
desired evil.

Tuggie's first step, literally, was to walk
over the snowy fields, the frozen roads, to
Bosum's house to obtain some twigs or sprigs
of withered grass that had grown and still

lingered in his dooryard. Lest Bosum's wife should suspect any uncanny motive for her visit, she carefully elaborated a plan, and carried on, in its furtherance, a long conversation with regard to a certain coveted dye-stuff which Mother Sidet manufactured; it turned all woollen stuffs a vivid green, and was in much demand throughout Narragansett to dye old woollen rags and worn-out flannel sheets and shirts this brilliant, verdant hue, when they could thereafter be used to most astonishing and satisfactory advantage in conferring variety in the manufacture of those triumphs of decorative art, those outlets of rural color-sense, home-made woven rag-carpets, and hooked and braided rugs. Tuggie argued with much dignity and volubility that she should be told the secret of this dye-stuff as some slight compensation for her ruined tea-kettle. It is needless to state that she was unsuccessful, nor had she expected to be otherwise. The secret of the dye was Molly Sidet's stock-in-trade, just as the soldering-iron and solder were her husband's.

At Molly's refusal Tuggie waxed wroth, and a most unpleasant exchange of personalities took place, which culminated in Tuggie's exasperating reference to an event which had occurred in Bosum's youth, and about which he and his wife were exceedingly and naturally sensitive. He had once gone proudly to Boston for a three months' visit to ply his trade and see the town. At the end of two weeks he had reappeared in Narragansett, kit in hand and depressed in appearance. When interrogated as to the reason of his sudden and speedy return, he had answered, acrimoniously, that "Boston folks is too full of notions." In the course of a few weeks, however, news came to Narragansett that Bosum had been arrested in Boston for his well-known trick of stealing, and had been whipped through the town at the cart-tail. Nothing could anger Molly Sidet more than a reference to "Boston notions." Tuggie used this thorn in the side with well-planned judiciousness and with the pleasing and wholly satisfactory result that Molly ordered her fiercely out of the house. This was precisely what she desired, for a witch cannot work a full, a thoroughly successful conjure on one who has always treated her well and kindly, and shown her due hospitality; hence old Tuggie, by Molly's abrupt expulsion of her from her house, was left free to work her wicked will.

Though Tuggie did not get the coveted dye-stuff, nor the recipe therefor, she did not return home empty-handed; she managed to pick without discovery a few leafless twigs from the great bush of southernwood that grew by the stone doorstep of Bosum Sidet's house, and she felt that her visit had not been in vain. Fortune favored her. As she passed the door of the tinker's barn she slipped in unobserved and clipped a few hairs from the tail of his cow. It would have been much better, much surer, to have had these hairs from Bosum's own head, but to aspire to a fibre of his close-cropped wool was useless.

As Tuggie Bannocks walked home over the crisp snow she muttered to herself with delight, and she glowered and scowled at the children as she passed the school-house at the corner, and they hooted and jeered at her in return, and called out, "Te-Rap, Te-Rap," which everyone knows is the greeting that witches cry out to each other.

She certainly was deemed a witch by her neighbors as well as the children. And this reputation was not accidental, it was jealously cultivated. She conformed her mien and behavior to all that was expected of a witch;

and she had been gifted by nature with one
feature which, much to her satisfaction, en-
abled her to exhibit convincing proofs of her
pretensions. She had two full rows of double
teeth (front teeth and all were double), which
could be displayed to telling and bewildering advantage to those who thought her
"just like other folks."

She did have some uncanny habits; some
that, a century previous, in a Puritan community, would have set her afloat to sink or swim.

She never sat upon stool or chair or settle
in anyone's house ; no one had ever seen her
seated save on a table or dresser or bed, or
even on a cradle-head—this to the painful
apprehension of the mother who owned the
cradle.   When spinning flax in one house
she sat on a saw-horse. She had not a chair
in her house, but there was an oaken chair-
moulding at the top of the wainscoting in
her spacious old kitchen ; and it was cur-
rently reported and believed that when she
was alone she perched or clung with her
heels on this moulding. The Newport chap-
man, Chepa Rose, told at the Ferry that he
saw her one night running round the room
on the moulding. But Chepa was not truth-
ful, so I do not believe it.

Tuggie dwelt alone in the ell part of an old gambrel-roofed house, which had seen better days, but was now deserted and sadly dilapidated, and was indeed in its main portion almost roofless. The ell, which contained the great raftered kitchen and two other rooms, was, however, tight and comfortable, and made a cheerful, picturesque home. Tuggie, who was strong and capable, worked for the farmers' wives around; dipped candles, made soap, spun yarn and wove carpets, brewed and salted; she also cultivated a little patch of land of her own, and knit stockings to sell, and was altogether a very thrifty, industrious person. She was in reality far more afraid of being bewitched than she was confident of bewitching, and that evening, as she prepared to "burn a project" to conjure old Bosum Sidet, she started at every sound, and turned her petticoats inside out, to keep off evil spirits, and at last hung a bag of egg-shells around her neck as a potent saving-charm.

She first mixed a little flour and water into dough and stirred in the hairs from the cow's tail — these were the straw for her brick; then she moulded the dough into the shape of a heart and stuck two pins in for

legs and two for arms; this would surely give
Bosum "misery in de legs and arms"—in
short, rheumatism.   This dough-heart she
set aside, for it was not properly part of
the project, and would only fulfil its diaboli-
cal mission when it was carried to Bosum's
door and set upon his fence or door-step,
when the "misery" would begin.

She then, with rather a quaking heart,
prepared to burn the project.   The sprigs of
southernwood from Bosum's door-yard, a few
rusty nails, the tail of a smoked herring, a
scrap of red flannel, a little mass of "grave-
dirt" that she had taken from one of the
many graveyards that are dotted all over
Narragansett, and, last of all, that chief in-
gredient, the prime factor in all negro charms
—a rabbit's foot—were thrown into a pot
of water that was hung upon the crane over
a roaring fire.   Of course everyone in Narragansett knew that when a project began to
boil the conjured one would begin to suffer
some mental or bodily ill; hence Tuggie
listened with much satisfaction to the pre-
monitory bubbling within the pot.

She stepped into the centre of the room on
account of the heat of the fire, and because
it is not good luck to watch a boiling proj-

ect; and as she stood in the red glow of
the firelight she was the personification of
negro superstition. Tall and gaunt, with
long bony arms, and skinny claws of hands,
with a wrinkled, malicious, yet half-fright-
ened countenance, surrounded by little pig-
tails of gray wool that stuck out from under
her scarlet turban, with her old petticoat
turned inside out, and a gay little shawl
pinned on her shoulders, she stood like a
Voodoo priestess eagerly watching and lis-
tening. When the boiling fairly began, she
commenced swaying, rocking herself backward and forward, patting the floor with
heavy foot, almost dancing while she muttered and sung, in a low voice, a few gib-
berish charms that had been taught by her
mother, Queen Abigail. She rolled her eyes
up in a superstitious ecstasy, and swung her
long arms to the rhythm of her heathenish
song, when suddenly a shock like an earth-
quake struck her door; it flew violently
open, and some long, heavy object rushed
in, struck Tuggie violently on her tender
shins, and threw her, face downward, on the
floor. She was for a moment stunned with
the fall and with the suddenness of the assault, but when she regained her senses she

still lay on the floor with eyes tightly closed
and her face covered with her hands, for
this violent assailant was surely that terrifying
creature, a " moonack," that she had raised
and brought by her wicked conjuring, and
if she glanced at it, it would cause her instant death.

Perfect stillness had succeeded the assault.
The old negress groaned and tried to pray.
She repeated some old Voodoo charms, the
Creed, all kinds of words to ward off evil
spirits, and at last pleaded aloud, "Oh, Mass'
Debbil, you only lets me go dis time, I won't
nebber burn no projects no more; I warn't
a-goin' to hurt Bosum anyway, I only wants
to git a new tea-kettle outen him.   I'll frow
de project out, and burn up de dough-baby,
an' lug back dat wool I stole from Debby
Nickkels, an' I won't nebber purtend I'se a
witch agin.   Oh! Mass' Moonack! Don't
take me dis time."   At this juncture she
again became speechless with terror, for
she heard soft, irregular footsteps entering
the door.   She groaned and moaned, but
did not open her eyes.

Four pale and staring boys, Tom and
Jeffrey Hazard, Zeke Gardiner, and Pel
Noyes, stole softly in on tiptoe, caught hold of

the clumsy caricature of a bob-sled that had so
fiercely assaulted Tuggie's shins and knocked
her down, dragged it out of the house and
disappeared with it down the road.   Jeffrey
Hazard, who had in him throughout his
entire life a far more active and real devil
than any evil spirit that Tuggie conjured or
dreamed of, could not resist, ere he left the
house, catching the old woman by the foot
as he passed her and pulling her as if to take
her off with him, until her groans of fright
made him desist.

Old Tuggie listened to the light footsteps
and the dragging noise in agony.   With
close-shut eyes she listened to the steps of the
devils and moonacks as they gradually went
away from the house.   The cold, icy night-
air blew in upon her as she lay on the floor,
the water burned down in the pot, and a
nauseous odor of burning fish and flesh filled
the house.   At last she tremblingly arose,
closed the door, swung the pot off the fire,
seized a horseshoe and prayer-book, and went
to bed.

The week previous Pel Noyes had been to
Boston, and had returned with his brain and
tongue full of a fine sled for coasting that he
had seen in that great metropolis.   With

four old sleigh-runners and a few boards he
had rigged an imitation of the beautiful
" double-runner," and the four boys sallied
out that winter night to use and enjoy it.
They intended to skim past Witch Tuggie's
door with a shrill and annoying shriek of de-
fiance, but alas ! their clumsy steering-ap-
paratus broke when they were half-way down
the hill, and the contrary sled, rudderless
and uncontrolled, instead of gliding past the
witch's door banged into it, with the full
success that we know. The boys were thrown
into the snow outside the door, and their
first impulse was to abandon their newly
manufactured sled and run for their lives;
but they were quick to discover, from manner
and word, that Tuggie was more frightened
than they were, and they stole in softly and
rescued the sled out of the very witch's den.

A BLACK POLITICIAN

A BLACK POLITICIAN

ON a bright June morning in the year
1811, old Cuddymonk sat in the cheerful
sunlight at the open door of his house, on
the banks of Lake Petaquamscut, in old
Narragansett. Cuddymonk was a negro;
but a Narragansett negro was, at that date,
of almost another race than a Southern
negro. He was free; he was usually re-
spected and self-respecting; he might, and
often did, own a house and farm of his own;
and he had a certain independent social position which was far from being a despised
one, for he enjoyed, with his rich white
neighbors, who had been slave-owners, a
friendly intimacy that was denied to a poor
white man. He was, however, somewhat
lazy, occasionally untruthful, and even dishonest—like his Southern colored brother.
Cuddymonk was a typical Narragansett
negro —sharp, shrewd, and in the main
thrifty. He was deeply and consistently

superstitious, and knew a thousand tales of
ghosts and spirits and witches and Manitous,
old traditions of African Voodooism and Indian pow-wows. He was profoundly learned
in the meaning of dreams and omens and
predictions, and he did not hesitate to practise—or attempt to practise—all kinds of
witch-charms and "conjures" and "projects," though he was a member in good
standing, as he proudly stated, of " de Pisti-
kle Church."

He was a good cobbler, a fair tinker, a
poor mason, a worse carpenter, a first-class
fisherman. He worked at any and all of
these trades with cheerful and indolent im-
partiality, just as he fiddled, and sheared
sheep, and ploughed, and sowed, and raked,
and harvested for his rich white neighbors;
but when anyone asked him his real trade,
he proudly answered, " I's er pollertishun."

He was indeed a politician, for he had
held the highest political position that his
State and race afforded : he had thrice been
elected " Black Gov'nor " of Narragansett
on "Nigger 'Lection Day "—not on account of his master's great wealth and high
position, as was in slavery times " Gov'nor "
Aaron Potter ; not for his military prowess,

as was "Gov'nor" Guy Watson, who had
served bravely at Ticonderoga and at the
absurd capture of General Prescott; not, as
was "Gov'nor" Prince Robinson, for his
handsome person and stately appearance,
for poor Cuddy possessed neither. He had
been elected just as white governors frequently are elected nowadays—because he was a
politician. His office, however, bore no
salary and but few emoluments; but it con-
ferred great honor and dignity, and through
it he received many small favors. He was
consulted as to the settlement of many petty
disputes among his black brothers, and his
decision was law. His office thus had a certain power, and commanded some respect
among the white people, who through him
could obtain small settlements and adjust-
ments, and arrange many matters in their
relations with the negroes, without the
trouble of personal effort. Cuddy had the
honor of having many of his legal decisions
and political aphorisms and his abstruse
financial opinions quoted at the white Governor's table, where they had been received
with much laughter, and some praise, also,
for their shrewdness.

His election had been a scene of great festivity. On the third Saturday in June (on which Nigger 'Lection was always held) there gathered in the great oak grove on Rose Hill the black inhabitants, riding on saddles and pillions, in chaises and farm-wagons, in ox-carts even—men, women, and children—all in their gayest and finest attire, from all the towns around. At ten o'clock the canvass commenced. Weeks of " 'lec-tureneerin' and parmenteerin'" had roused great interest in the event, and at last the two rows of the male friends of the respective candidates were arranged in lines under the trees in the charge of two pompous marshals, while the women stood admiringly around. Cuddymonk, mounted on Colonel Gardiner's gray horse, and wearing a fine coat and knee-breeches that had been given him by the colonel, with a great borrowed gold-laced cocked hat balanced on the back of his head, rode up and down the line flourishing a long sword that had been lent him for the occa-sion. And he kept quiet and order, that no one might change ranks after the counting began, or step from one end of the line to the other, and thus fraudulently increase the number of votes. When the counting was done the number of votes and successful

candidate was announced. Cuddymonk's
election was received with tumultuous cheers
and congratulations.

Only one event occurred to mar the dignity of this first election. As he was about
to end his inauguration address with a glorious flourish and climax of ornate rhetoric,
his defeated opponent called out, in a high,
malicious voice, " Cuddy, yer calfs has got
round in front ! " Cuddy glanced down at
his legs with apprehensive mortification.
Alas ! it was too true. Colonel Gardiner
had given with the knee-breeches a pair of
his fine long stockings : but as he was as
sturdy and muscular as Cuddy was thin, and
as the politician had even more " negative
calf and convex shin " (as said Randolph of
Virginia) than have most of his race, the
colonel's stockings hung in unsightly folds ; '
that Cuddy's wife, Rosann, remedied by
thrusting into each stocking-leg a great roll
of sheep's wool. In the heat of " parmenteerin'," and through constant friction against
his horse's sides, Cuddy's woollen calves had
indeed " got round in front." In vain did
he try, amid the jeers of his opponents, to re-
place the unsightly wads in a dignified and
proper position ; they refused to stay placed,

and for the rest of the day, at the dinner
and at the dance, the false calves hung in
front of and under his sharp old knees, looking for all the world, in the gray, wrinkled
stockings, like a pair of hornets' nests under
the eaves of a house.

It may plainly be seen that by virtue of
his position old Cuddymonk was of the high
aristocracy of Narragansett black society.
He was also an aristocrat by birth. The
blood of African kings ran in his veins, and
a strong cross of Indian blood, that of old
King Ninigret, showed in his high cheek-
bones and coarse black hair. His skin,
too, was far from black. As he sat in the
clear sunlight on this May morning, his bare
feet and hands and face were of a uniform
glowing golden-brown color, as rich and
cheerful, though not as orange-tinted, as a
ripe pumpkin. The appearance of his head
was, also, most unlike the wool-covered,
low-browed, heavy-jawed cranium of a negro ; for his half-curly, coarse hair grew on
the back part of his head only, and stuck
out in a great stiff, surrounding halo. The
top and sides of his head being thus left
bare gave to him the appearance of having
an extraordinarily high and brain-developed

forehead ; and altogether these peculiarities caused him to bear a comical cranial resemblance both to the noble Shakespeare and a blue-haired, ring-crowned baboon. His teeth and eyeballs showed the brilliant, glittering white of the negro, not at all like the dingy black snags and reddish, inflamed eyeballs seen in the Indian. He wore a collarless and rather ragged white shirt, an ancient and much-worn long-tailed blue coat with brass buttons, the very coat which had been given to him by Colonel Gardiner to attire him fitly and gloriously upon his election as "Gov'nor." But the garment having served through three terms of office (to say nothing of the many years it had faithfully covered the colonel's back), was now degraded to every-day wear. Cuddy was also clad in a shapeless pair of loose yellowish tow trousers called "tongs," that bore strong evidence not only of home spinning and weaving, but of home tailoring as well, if such unsightly great linen bags could be said to be tailored.

Cuddy regarded with much satisfaction a row of dilapidated beehives that stood by his door, whose busy inhabitants furnished to him the toothsome honey he so dearly loved,

and which he could so readily and profitably
sell when he could "spare" it. He looked
with equal pride on a row of thriving okra-
plants, whose long green pods would in
midsummer make for him such succulent and
nourishing soups, and would also be sliced
into delicate pale green, six-rayed stars, and
displayed for weeks on window-sills and
door-stones and shed-tops and stone walls in
his small domain, through sunny, windless
days when the starry wafers would not be
blown away, drying for his own winter use
and to carry to Newport to sell.   His only
other crop was represented by a freshly
turned plot of earth—a potato-field—which
he had planted the previous day.

Cuddymonk stretched himself with delight
in the sunshine, and thus spoke to his wife,
Rosann, a gay-turbaned old woman, who
was twice as fat and twice as black as he
was:

"I tell ye, Rosann, 'tatoes an' honey an'
okra is a tousan' times better'n pigs; ye
don' have ter feed 'em, an' tend 'em, and
watch 'em eaten theirselves up. Dey jess
grows an' grows for nothin'. Ef more folks
growed 'tatoes an' okra in dis country,
times'd be better'n dey is."

Rosann did not answer him, she seldom did ; and now her attention was called to a horse and rider that had turned from the main road and were advancing up the narrow lane that led to Cuddy's house. Mounted visitors were not frequent at Cuddy's humble home, even on gubernatorial business; and when he and Rosann saw that the horseman was no less a person than Constable Cranston, of North Kingston, they stared in open-mouthed amazement. No less astonished were they when the sheriff announced his errand—that he had come to arrest the "Gov'nor" for debt. Suit had been brought against him and judgment rendered, and his arrest was the next step.

For Cuddymonk, like many another philosopher and many another politician, was careless and even tricky in business matters, and had been accused by both black and white neighbors of "never paying fer nothing if he could help it." That he should have been arrested for this special debt was to him most astonishing, and he denounced it as keen injustice. He thus protested to the sheriff :

"Mass' Cranston, yer don't know what yer a-doin'. I don't owe ole man Hazard

nothin'! Yer see, it was jess like dis. I
say ter him, I mus' hab er pig ter raise.
He say ter me, 'Take one ob mine;' an'
he press me ter take it, kase it's a runtlin',
an' he's afear'd it'll die. An' Rosann, she
knows how ter mother runtlin's, so I takes
der pig. An' I say, 'Ole man Hazard, I
pay you free dollar ob de money I git for
der pig.' He say, 'All right, Cuddy.'
Now I don't nebber git no money fer dat
pig. I buy de corn ter feed der pig of Peleg
Brown; an' when I kill de pig an' take him
ter Peleg ter sell, he don' come ter ser much
as de corn he eat. I t'ink he shrink kase I
kill him in de discrease ob de moon. So I
nebber got nothin' fer de pig, so in course
I don' owe ole man Hazard nothin'. I
ain't got no money ter pay wid, anyway.
I tell ye, Mass' Cranston, times nebber'll be
good in dis country till corn's a pistareen a
bushel an' pork a pistareen a pound. Den
de pore man'll hab some chance.''

Mr. Cranston knew old Cuddy too well
to allow him to proceed into the discussion
of political economy; and he interrupted
the "Gov'nor," saying, with much gravity,
that the law must take its course, nor could
the execution of justice be delayed; that

since Cuddy could not pay, he must come at once with him to jail. The negro rose cheerfully, saying, as he hobbled into the house:

"Wal, ef I mus' go I mus'; but de exertootion ob justice'll hab to move mighty slow a-takin' ole Cuddy ter jail. I'se got der rheumatiz, so I can't hardly walk. I'se dat bad I t'inks I mus' be witch-rid by ole Tuggie Bannocks. Dat's why dat pig eat ser much corn kase she conjured him. Times nebber'll be good in dis country whiles dey don' hang ole witches like Tuggie Bannocks. Hitch yer hoss ter de button-wood tree an' come in an' set down while I'se packin' up, an' Rosann'll cook ye some early 'tatoes. Run out an' git some of our first crap, Sanna."

"Early potatoes!" exclaimed Mr. Cranston, "at this time of the year!"

"Yis, I'se a fust-rate farmer, ef I ain't much on pig-raisin'. I allays has fine early 'tatoes, de fust yer see anywheres. Jes' look at dem!"

Rosann appeared with her apron full of the freshly planted potatoes, that, negrofashion, he had planted whole, and that had spent a few hours only on Cuddy's farm;

and as the sheriff refused to allow her to cook them for him, she placed them upon a blanket in the centre of the floor, upon which she and Cuddy were accumulating the articles that the negro wished to take to jail with him.   The pile rapidly increased.   Old coats and shirts, a feather pillow, a fiddle, a prayer-book, a pair of long boots filled with flax-seed, were added to the contents of the blanket.

"Come, come," said the sheriff; "you can't take all that along with you.   How are you going to carry it?"

"I guess you'll hab ter tote it for me, Mass' Cranston, I'se dat bad wid the rheumatiz."

This was more than the constable had bargained for.   This arrest of old Cuddy was more than half a joke, and was done at the instigation of several farmers who hoped thus to obtain some satisfaction for the many debts Cuddy had argued and twisted himself out of paying.   They had all fancied that the terrified politician would gladly pay over the three dollars at once, as it was well known that Rosann had a good stockingful of silver dollars hidden under the hearth-stone—and one of her stockings full of silver was well worth having. The constable was on his way to attend to other and more pressing duties, and had but little time to spend over this arrest ; much less did he wish to ride to Kingston jail carrying a great pack of Cuddy-monk's clothing and possessions behind him. He told Rosann to remove half of the articles from the blanket, and a long and wordy argument with the " Gov'nor " arose over every relinquished treasure, ending in the constable's complete rout when he attempted to leave the foot-stove behind and to pour the flax-seed out of his boots. "I can't do dat, noway," said Cuddy ; "it'll spoil deir shape ef I don' keep flax-seed in 'em, an I'se afeard I can't get none in jail." At the end of half an hour the blanket with its contents was rolled into a great, irregular, unwieldy bundle and strapped on the horse's back.

The man of law mounted his horse, and with his prisoner passed slowly down the narrow lane and through the rocky cross-road under the feathery pale-green foliage and sweet-scented pink-and-white blossoms of the graceful locust-trees that form such a glory in early summer by all the roadsides throughout sunny Narragansett. Flickering patches of glowing sunlight fell through the clusters of peachy locust-blossoms on the stone walls and hedgerows, that were a great, luxuriant, tangled garden of faintly perfumed wild flowers. The leaves of sweetbrier and bayberry sent out a pungent, spicy odor that mingled with the vapid and cloying sweetness of the locust-blossoms. Great fields of clover wafted their fresh balm in little puffs of pure sweetness that routed the combined fragrance of locust, bayberry, and brier. Thousands of bees hummed over the sweet, sunny fields and in the fragrant, flowering branches—Cuddy's own bees gathering for him the luscious honey he loved. Singing-birds flew lightly and warbled softly around. The tropical blood of the old negro fairly glowed with the sense of light and perfume and melody and warmth, and he laughed aloud with sensuous delight as if the road to jail lay through Paradise.

He hobbled painfully, however, even in the warm sunlight, and he frequently sat down on a sunny stone to rest his rheumatic old bones; but his tongue never ceased wagging, and he poured forth to the constable a flood of political, ethical, physical, legal, spiritual, meteorological, thaumaturgical, and medical advice, and also a complete local

history of past events in Narragansett. A
flame of youth and memory and happiness
seemed kindled by the glorious summer day
in his heart and brain, though his poor body
was too stiff and worn to renew also its activity and youth.

At last he said, smilingly, to the constable:
" Mass' Cranston, ef you'll go de ribber road
an' wants ter let me stop ter Kernel Gardiner's I kin get some money; he owes me five
dollar for honeycomb."

Gladly did Sheriff Cranston consent,
though Colonel Gardiner's house was two
miles out of the way, for he saw now a pros-
pect of release from his cumbersome charge.
" Here, Cuddy," he said, " we sha'n't get
to the Colonel's for two hours at this rate—
you talk so much and walk so little. You
get up and ride and I'll walk for awhile,
then we shall get along faster."

The old negro, with the constable's assistance, mounted and smiled with delight; for
he loved a horse, as do all of his race. A
gleam of humor twinkled in his eye as he
urged on the sturdy sorrel, a half-blooded
Narragansett pacer, until she ambled along
at a rate that forced the constable to walk at
an uncomfortably rapid and perspiring pace.

Nor was Mr. Cranston altogether comfortable mentally. He winced several times in his progress at the laughing inquiries and jeers of the farmers that he saw in the field or passed in the road; and the shouts of the district-school children at the "Corner," who chanced to be "out at recess" as the "Black Gov'nor" and his white foot-runner coursed along, made him keenly conscious that the dignity of the law was not fully preserved, either in his hurrying, panting figure or in the grotesque appearance of short-legged Cuddy. For the Narragansett pacer, like others of her race, was phenomenally broad-backed; and Cuddy's short, stiff legs, clad in their unsightly, flapping tow tongs, stuck out at an absurd angle, showing a long expanse of skinny, bare ankles that looked like yellow turkey-legs; and the enormous uncurried leather shoes that he had donned, in which to walk in comfort to jail, looked twice as large as ever in that prominent position. The constable had an uneasy suspicion that Cuddy had retained his tow tongs and long-tailed coat, and had put on his old black satin brass-buckled stock and red woollen comforter and great moth-eaten fur cap—the worst clothes he had in the world—in order to look as

ridiculous as possible, and thus guy his cap-
tor. But the cheerful yellow countenance
of the prisoner bore not a trace of any possi-
bility of ever cherishing a sinister design.

When they reached the great gambrel-
roofed house of Colonel Gardiner the negro
dismounted and entered. He soon reappeared, saying, cheerfully, "I'se got de
money, Mass' Cranston."

"Hurry up, then, and give me the three
dollars," said the constable, impatiently. "I
want to get off."

The negro stared in astonishment: "I
ain't agoin' ter spen' dat honey-money dat
way—payin' fer an ole dead pig I don' owe
nothin' fer. I'se goin' to keep it ter be
comferable in jail wid. Didn' yer hear Rosann say, 'Keep comferable, Cuddy?' Dat's
why I brung de foot-stove fer!"

The constable was wild with indignation
and disgust. He had gone two miles out of
his way—painfully running and perspiring
while his prisoner rode at ease—and now he
was farther from the end of his vexatious
business than ever. He impatiently explained
and argued to the stubborn negro that if he
would only pay over part of the five dollars
he would need no jail comforts. Still the old

man was persistent in his determination; he had started to go to jail, and to jail he would go.

"I ain't agoin' ag'inst de course ob de law. It 'ud be a pretty scandal fer de Gub'nor not ter go ter jail when he 'rested. Set ebberybody a bad edsample. I'se er lawerbidin' citterzman, an' I'se goin' ter 'bey de law ob de lan'. B'sides, Rosann she say she t'inks I get red ob my rheumatiz' in jail. Ole Tuggie Bannocks can't get me out nights ter witch-ride me."

The discomfited sheriff at last rode slowly on, while Cuddy again hobbled alongside, still cheerful, still philosophizing, still advising. Mr. Cranston was puzzled. He could not abandon his prisoner, nor could he persuade or force him to pay the debt; still less could he hurry him, and the time to perform other and more important duties was close at hand. At last, completely baffled and conquered, he suddenly exclaimed: "Here, Cuddymonk, I've had enough of this; take your bundle, I'll pay your debt to old Hazard and the costs, too."

"Mass' Cranston, is dat de way yer does yer duty? I'se agoin' ter jail ef I hab ter walk dere alone, an' tell de jedge dat de constable run off an' leff me. I ain't no runnagadore. I'se goin' in de cause ob de right. You'se 'rested me, an' I'se agoin' ter stay 'rested. I nebber see a jail, anyway, an' I wants ter see one. Times neber'll be good in dis country till bof people an' rulers knows erbout de instertootions ob de lan'!''

Again did the baffled sheriff explain and expostulate and seek to rouse in Cuddy a sense of pride and dread of shame. "It's most time for 'Lection Day, Cuddy. You'll never be elected again if you go to jail. They'll never want a rogue for Gov'nor.''

" 'Cause de Gov'nor am a rogue this year ain't no sign de next one won't be,'' answered wise Cuddy. And when the constable had straightened out Cuddy's ambiguous thought, he said to himself that black politics were much like white.

"I can't see why all you blacks are so dishonest and tricky!''

"Why, Mass' Cranston " (with an injured but unresentful air), "dey has ter be —dey so kep' down. It all de fault ob dat unrageous ole George Washin'ton. When he a-dyin he rolls his eyes an' say : 'Forebber keep de nigger down'—an' it take a hundred year to work out a dyin' spell.''

This astounding piece of post-mortem

news about the Father of his Country was
new to the constable, though it was commonly believed by negroes then as now. He
answered Cuddy severely and sharply :

"Who told you that nonsense ?   It's no
reason, anyway.   There is no need for any
nigger to be dishonest unless he wants to."

" Now, Mass' Cranston, dis' jess de way
I looks at it.   Times nebber'll be good in
dis country till things is fixed an' proputty's
divided so no one can't be poor ; den no one
can't be dishonest, cause ef dey has plenty
dey won't want ter be."

The constable felt that it was useless to
argue further with such a philosopher, and
rode on for some time in silence ; then he
desperately exclaimed: " Cuddy, what'll
you take to go home again ?   I can't bother
any longer with you.   I've got to go to
Wickford to-night, and you can't walk
there."

The old negro shook his head profoundly and thoughtfully, and sighed deeply, as
though abandoning with keen regret a dearly loved and cherished plan; then he said,
solemnly :

" No bribe'll ebber soil dis hand while it
fills de office ob de Gub'nor's seat !   But

dey do say de best charm eber seed ter
bring good luck forebber is ter look at a
constable a-dancin' ober runnin' water.
Now here's de bridge an' a good dancin'-
floor. I'll hole der hoss an' sing ' Old
Charmany Fair,' an' you dance, ter bring
good luck ter me in de 'lection next week.
Den I s'pose I'll hab ter gib up going ter
jail dis time just ter please yer."

The constable was stunned by this auda-
cious and fairly insulting proposition ; but
being thoroughly convinced that Cuddy was
half demented, he thought it better to yield
at once to the stubborn negro's condition,
and thus save his precious and much-wasted
time. He jumped from his horse and
angrily yanked off Cuddy's blanketful of
jail equipage, and threw it on the ground.
He glanced apprehensively up and down the
road to see that there was no approaching
traveller to spread the tale of his ridiculous
discomfiture and abject submission, and then
walked to the middle of the bridge and began to sullenly dance to Cuddy's lively and
rollicking dance-tune. The jolly song and
dismal jig were nearly ended, when a most
surprising and inexplicable event took place.
The constable's sedate and quiet horse gave

a sudden snort, reared, broke away from
Cuddy's restraining hand, and plunged violently down the hill.

"Stop her! Stop her, Cuddy!" roared
Mr. Cranston, as he suddenly ceased his
forced dance and began to run.

"I ain't agoin' ter run none after dat ole
hoss," said Cuddy; "I'se got de rheumatiz'
too bad. You jess see ef you can't run
faster as you can dance. You can't catch
her, dough," he called after the retreating
sheriff. "I know she's conjured by de way
she run. It always do conjure a hoss to see
a constable a-dancin' ober runnin' water."

As the constable shouted "Whoa!" at the
top of his lungs and chased wildly down the
hill out of sight, Cuddy walked to the side of
the bridge and threw into the water the long,
sharp locust-thorn that had done such sly
and good execution as a spur, as a "conjure" to the sheriff's steed. Then he sat
down by the side of his blanket bundle in the
hot noonday sunlight, and he took out his
fiddle and scraped and sawed to the bees
and birds and butterflies like a jolly yellow
Pan. And he chuckled and laughed and
whistled and sang, and once he jumped up
and danced through "Old Chalmouni Fair"

with a brisk vigor that put to shame the unwilling and clumsy efforts of the constable,
and made the tow tongs and the blue coat-
tails snap and flap around his shrivelled old
yellow legs.   It was certainly most astonishing to see such agility and activity in a man
so aged, and in one so rheumatic and so
witch-ridden an hour previously.   At last a
passing farm-wagon picked him up and carried him and his great bundle to his own
door.

As Cuddymonk replanted his early potatoes the following morning, he once more
soliloquized to his wife :

"I tell you, Rosann, dat ole fool ob a
Cranston won't nebber 'rest me fer debt no
more.   I ain't goin' to raise no more pigs
anyway, even ef I does get 'em somewhat
cheap.   'Tatoes is better'n pigs.   Times
nebber'll be good in dis country till ebberybody stops raisin' pigs an' plant 'tatoes;
dat's de true secret ob de pollitercul crisis
ob dis land."

THE WITCH SHEEP

THE WITCH SHEEP

In the darkness of Christmas morning, in the year 1811, old Benny Nichols could not sleep. He was not thinking of Santa Claus nor of Christmas gifts; he was watching for the first gray dawn which marked his regular rising hour, and he tossed and turned, wondering why he was so wakeful, until at last he rose in despair and lighted a candle to discover how long he had to wait ere daybreak. To his amazement he found the hands of the old clock pointing to the hour of nine, and as he stood shivering, candle in hand, staring at the apparently deceitful, bland face the clock raised its voice and struck nine, loudly and brassily, as if to prove that its hands and face told the truth. Benny then walked quickly to the window, and saw that the apparent darkness and length of the night came from a great wall of snow which covered the entire window and which had nearly all fallen since the previous sunset.

Keenly awake at once when he recognized the lateness of the hour, the old man wakened his wife Debby, and bade her "hurry up and git somethin' to eat. It's nine o'clock, and we've had the wust snowstorm ye ever see, and me a-laying' here in bed, and them new sheep a-walkin' into the sea and gittin' drownded!"

Benny was a weazened-faced, dried-up old man, who was the shepherd of a large Narragansett farm which lay between Pender Zeke's Corner and the bay. He knew well the danger that came to sheep in a heavy snowstorm. He had seen a great flock of a hundred timid, shrinking creatures retreat and cower one behind the other to shelter themselves from the fierce beating of the wind and sleet, until, in spite of his efforts, all were edged into the sea and lost, save a half-dozen whose throats were cut by him with a jack-knife to save the mutton. Without waiting for any warm food, he cautiously opened the door to dig himself out.

"Ye can't go out, Benny Nichols, in them shoes," said Debby, firmly. "I told

ye long ago they was half wore out—here,
put on yer Sunday long-boots."

This suggestion was a bitter one to pru-
dent Benny, who expected to have those
boots for Sunday wear for the next ten
years, just as he had for the past ten ; and
he knew well what a hard day's work he
had before him, and how destructive it
would prove to shoe-leather. But Debby
was firm, and, seizing the great boots from
the nail on which they hung, she poured
out the flax-seed with which they were always kept filled when they were not on
Benny's feet. The old man pulled them
on his shrivelled legs with a groan at Debby's extravagance, and then proceeded to
dig out a path in the snow. Benny had
not seen such a snow-storm since the great
"Hessian snow-storm" in the winter of
1778, when so many Hessian soldiers per-
ished of cold and exposure. When he
reached the surface and could look around
him, he saw with satisfaction that the snow
and wind had blown during the previous
night *away* from the water, hence his sheep
would hardly be drowned. He quickly
discovered a strange-shaped bank of snow
by the side of one of the great hay-ricks,

so common throughout Narragansett, and he shrewdly suspected that some of his sheep were underneath the great drift. When carefully searched with a rake-stale this proved to be the case, and when he shovelled them out all in the mound were alive and well. In a snow-drift, by the side of a high stone wall, he found the remainder of his flock, save one, a fine little ewe of the creeper breed, the rarest and most valued of all his stock. As sheep-sheds at that time were unknown in Narragansett, the loss of sheep was great in the Christmas storm, and many cattle were frozen in the drifts; and one shepherd noted two weeks later that the hungry cattle he foddered never touched a full lock of hay that he had thrown on the top of a little hillock of snow near his rick. So he thrust at it with his hay-tines, and in so doing he lifted off a great shell of snow-crust, and there peered out of the whiteness the bronze, wrinkled face of the old squaw Betty Aaron, who was sitting bolt upright, frozen stiff and dead, her chin resting on both hands, her elbows on her knees. Hence Benny was justly proud of his rescued flock, though he mourned the one sheep

that was lost, and blamed himself for sleeping so late, saying, he "wouldn't have
minded spilin' his roast-meat boots if he
could have found the creeper."

On the fourteenth day of January Benny
Nichols chanced to see in the snow, by the
side of a hay-rick which stood a mile away
from his home, a small hole about half an
inch in diameter, which his practised eye
recognized at once as a "breathing-hole,"
and which indicated that some living
thing had been snowed in and was lying
underneath. He broke away the covering
of icy crust, and to his amazement saw a
poor creature of extraordinary appearance,
which he at first hardly could believe was
his own lost creeper sheep. She was alive,
but alas! in such a sorry plight.

The hungry sheep, in her three weeks'
struggle against starvation, had eaten off
every fibre of her own long wool that she
could reach, and she lay bare and trembling in the cold air, too weak to move,
too feeble to bleat either in distress or
welcome. Old Benny wrapped the half-
dead creature in the corner of his cloak
and carried her home to Debby, who fairly
shed tears at the sight of the poor naked

skeleton of a sheep. Tenderly did the kind woman wrap the frozen ewe in an old flannel petticoat and feed her with warm milk, a few drops only at first, and then with much caution until the sheep was able to digest her ordinary food. In a week the creeper seemed as strong as ever, quickly gained the lost flesh, and could bleat both loud and long. And with returning health she grew active and mischievous, and was constantly thrusting her long black nose into the most unexpected and most unsuitable places, to the great distress of careful Debby, who longed to put her out of doors.

But the sheep's lost wool could not grow as quickly as did the fat on her ribs, and she could not be thrust out thus, naked and bare, in the winter air, so Debby decided to make for the little creature a false fleece. For this purpose she took an old blue coat which had once been worn by her son, and cut off the sleeves until they were the right length to cover the ewe's forelegs. She then sewed at the waist of the coat two sleeves from an old red flannel shirt; these were to cover Nanny's hind legs. And when Debby drew on the gay jacket and buttoned it up over the sheep's long backbone with the large brass coat-buttons, there never was seen such a comical, stunted, hind-side-foremost caricature of what is itself a caricature—an organ-grinder's monkey.

When Benny carried the gayly dressed Nanny out to the enclosed yard, it was hard to tell which exhibition of feeling was the keenest—poor, unconscious, and absurd Nanny's delight in her freedom and her eager desire to take her place with her old companions, or the consternation and terror of the entire flock at the strange wild beast which was thus turned loose among them.

They ran from side to side, and crowded each other against the paling so unceasingly and so wildly, that Benny carried the unwilling ewe back to the kitchen.

At nightfall, however, Benny again placed Nanny in the open field with the sheep, thinking that they would gradually, throughout the darkness, become used to the presence of her little harlequin jacket, and allow her to graze by their side in peace.

That night two cronies of Benny's came from a neighboring farm to talk over that ever-interesting topic, the great snowstorm, and to buy some of his lambs. The three

old men sat by the great fireplace in the old
raftered kitchen in the pleasant glow from
the blazing logs, each sipping with unction
a mug of Benny's famous flip, while Debby
rubbed with tallow the sadly stiffened long-
boots that had been worn in the Christmas
snow. Suddenly a loud wail of distress
rang in their ears, the door was thrust violently open, and in stumbled the breathless
form of the tall, gaunt old negress Tuggie
Bannocks. She was a relic of old slavery
times, who lived on a small farm near the
old Gilbert Stuart Mill, on Petaquamscut
River. They all knew her well. She had
bought many a pound of wool from Benny
to wash and card and spin into yarn, and
she always helped Debby in that yearly trial
of patience and skill—her soap-making. The
old negro woman had double qualifications
to make her of use in this latter work : her
long, strong arms could stir the soap untir-
ingly for hours, and then she knew also how
to work powerful charms—traditional relics
of Voodooism—to make the soap always turn
out a success.

Tuggie Bannocks sank upon the table
by the fire, murmuring : " Tanks be to
Praise ! Tanks be to Praise! " and closed

her eyes in speechless exhaustion. Debby took a half-crushed basket of eggs from the old woman's arm, drew off her red woollen mittens, and rubbed briskly her long cold claws of hands. Benny had a vague remembrance of the old-time "emergency" saying, "feathers for fainters," and seized a turkey's wing that was in daily use as a hearthbrush, thrust it into the flames, and then held the scorching feathers under the old negress's nose until all in the room were coughing and choking with the stifling smoke.

Spluttering and choking at the dense feather-smoke, Tuggie gasped out : "I ain't dead yit—I specks I shall be soon, dough—kase I seen de ole witch a-ridin'—I'se most skeered to death " (then in a fainter voice) —"gib me a mug of dat flip." Startled, Benny quickly drew a great mug of home-brewed beer and gave it a liberal dash of Jamaica rum and sugar, then seized from the fire the red-hot "loggerhead " and thrust it seething into the liquid until the flip boiled and bubbled and acquired that burnt, bitter flavor that he knew Tuggie dearly loved. The old woman moaned and groaned as she lay on the table-top, but watched the brewing of the flip with eager eye, and sat up with alacrity to drink it.

With many a shuddering sigh and many a glance behind her at the kitchen door, and crossing her fingers to ward off evil spirits she began : " Ye know, Miss Nickkels, I telled ye I was witch-rid by ole Mum Amey, an' dis how I know I was. Ye see I was a-goin' to wuk a charm on her first off—not to hurt her none, jess to bodder her a leetle—an' I jess put my project on de fire one night, an' it jess a-goin' to boil, an' in come her ugly, ole grinnin' black face at de door, an' say she a-goin' to set wid me a spell." Mum Amey was a wrinkled half-breed Indian of fabulous age and crabbed temper, a " squaw-nurse," who was, of course, not half as black as negro Tuggie. " She walk ober to de chimbly to light her pipe an' ask me what I a-cookin', an' I say Ise a-makin' glue, cause Ise afeard she see de rabbit's foot in de pot, an' I say it all done, an' yank de pot offen de crane so she can't see into it. An' ob course when I take de project offen de fire afore it's wukked, it break de charm ; an' wuss still, I can't nebber try no project on her no more. Ole Mum Amey larf, an' say, a-leerin' at me, dat pot ob glue won't nebber

stick nothin' no more. An' ebber sence dat
night I ben witch-rid. Mornin's when I
wakes up I sees marks ob de bit in de corners ob my mouf, where Mum Amey ben
a-ridin' me all ober Boston Neck an' up de
Ridge Hill till I so tired and stiff I can't
hardly move. Ise ben pinched in de night
an' hab my ha'r pulled. An' my butter
won't come till I drops a red-hot horseshoe
in de cream to dribe her out. One day I
jess try her to see ef she a witch (dough I
know she one, 'cause I see her talkin' to a
black cat); I drop a silber sixpence in her
path, an' jess afore she get to it she turn an'
go back, jess I know she would. No witch
can't step ober silber. An' now, Benny
Nickkels, I know for shore she's a witch, I
see her jess now in de moonlight a-chasin'
an' ridin' your sheep; an', shore's yer
bawn, yer'll find some on 'em stone dead in
de mornin'—all on 'em, mebbe ! "

Benny looked wretched enough at this
statement. Dearly as he loved his sheep and
ready as he was to face physical discomfort
and danger in their behalf, he was too superstitious to dare to go out in the night to
rescue them and brave the witch.

"How did she look, Tuggie? And

what did she do?" whispered awe-struck
Debby.

"Oh, she was mons'ous fearsome to see!
Witches don't nebber go in deir own form
when dey goes to deir Sabbaths. She was
long an' low like a snake. She run along de
groun' jess like a derminted yeller painter,
a-boundin', an' leapin', an' springin', a-
chasin' dem pore sheeps—oh, how dey run!
Wid her old red an' blue blanket tied tight
aroun' her—dat's how I knowed her. An'
she had big sparklin' gold dollars on her
back—wages ob de debbil, I 'specks. Sometimes she jump in de air an' spread her
wings an' fly awhile. Smoke an' sparks
come outen her mouf an' nostrums! Big
black horns stick outen her head! Lash her
long black tail jess like de debbil hisself!"

At this dramatic and breathless point in
Tuggie's flip-nourished and quickly growing
tale, credulous Debby, whose slow-working
brain had failed to grasp all the vivid details
in the black woman's fervid and imaginative
description, interjected this gasping com-
ment: "It must ha' been the devil or the
creeper."

Benny jumped from his chair and stamped
his foot, and at once burst into a loud laugh

of intense relief, and with cheerful bravado began to explain animatedly to his open-mouthed cronies that of course anyone could see that Tuggie's sheep-chasing witch was only the creeper sheep in her new fleece, and he offered swaggeringly to go out alone to the field to bring the ewe in to prove it.

The old negress sprang to her feet, insulted and enraged at the jeering laughter and rallying jokes, and advanced threateningly toward him. Then, as if with a second thought, she stopped with a most malicious look, and in spite of Debby's conciliatory explanations and her soothing expressions "that it might have been Mum Amey after all," she thrust aside Benny's proffered mollification of a fresh mug of flip, seized her crushed basket, stalked to the door, and left the house muttering, vindictively: "High time to stop such unrageous goin's-on—dressin' up sheeps like debbils—scarin' an ole woman to death an' breakin' all her aigs! Ole Tuggie Bannocks ain't forgot how to burn a project! Guess dey won't larf at witches den!"

And surely enough—as days passed it could plainly be seen that the old negress had carried out her threat—for the chimney

was "conjured" — was "salted." On
windy nights the shepherd and his wife were
sure they could hear Tuggie dancing and
stamping on the roof, and she blew down
smoke and threw down soot, and she called
down the chimney in a fine, high, shrieking
voice: "I'll project ye, Benny; I'll project ye." And she burnt the cakes before
the fire, and the roast upon the spit, and
thrice she snapped out a blazing coal and
singed a hole in Debby's best petticoat,
though it was worn wrong side out as
a saving-charm. And Benny could see,
too, that the old ram was bewitched. The remainder of the flock soon became accustomed to the sight of Nanny's funny false
fleece, but he always fled in terror at her approach. He grew thin and pale (or at any
rate faded), and he would scarcely eat when
Nanny was near. Debby despairingly tried a
few feeble counter-charms, or "warders," but
without avail. When sheep-shearing time
came, however, and Nanny, shorn of her uncanny fleece and clothed in her own half-
inch snowy wool, took her place with the
other short-clipped members of the flock, he
ceased to be "witch-rid"—the "project,"
the "conjure" was worked out. He grew

fat and fiercely brave, and became once more the knight of the field, the lord of the domain, the patriarch, the potestate of his flock.

The story of Tuggie Bannocks's fright and her revengeful " project " spread far and wide on every farm from Point Judith to Pottawomat, and was told in later years by one generation of farmers to another. And as time rolled on and Nanny reared her lambs and they her grand-lambs, the creeper sheep were known and sold throughout Narragansett by the name of witch-sheep.

THE
CRUSOES OF THE NOON-HOUSE

THE
CRUSOES OF THE NOON-HOUSE

In a grass-grown graveyard by the side of
an old Presbyterian church in Narragansett,
the warm, midday sun shone brightly down
one spring Sabbath in the year 1760 upon
two boys twelve years of age, two cousins,
named Elam Noyes and Cotton Fayerweather.
They stood by the side of their grandfather's
grave, which bore a new blue slate head-
stone, inscribed with his name and age, and
the verses :

> " You children of ye name of Noyes
> Make Jesus Christ yo'r oleny choyse."

The boys had gone into the church-yard
with the apparent design of examining this
fine, though misspelled, token of the stone-
cutter's art, but were really speaking and
thinking of a very different subject. They
would never have been allowed to wander in
the church-yard to indulge in idle talk, and
even now could spend but a few minutes in

conversation together. It was their only meeting-time during the week, for they lived at extreme ends of the town, and Elam recited his lessons to the Baptist minister, who lived near him, while Cotton attended the village school. They were two well-built, healthy boys, both dressed in clumsy, homespun suits of clothes, with full knee-breeches, long-flapped coats and waistcoats, coarse yarn stockings and buckled shoes, and great gray beaver hats several sizes too large for them. Elam was as solemn and serious in his appearance as was his father, but in his brain was a current of keen romance rarely found in the head of any elderly colonist. As he left the church-yard with his cousin he said, with much impressiveness, "Remember, Cotton, if you are not here by candle-light I shall tarry no longer, but shall go home."

For several Sundays, as the boys had walked among the graves, and while they had been busy with the care of their fathers' horses, Elam had occupied every moment in telling to Cotton all that he could remember of a wonderful story he had read in New Haven. Two months previously he had ridden with his father to that

town, and in the tap-room of the "ordinary" at which they had "put up" during
their stay there had lain a pile of about forty
books, which a sea-captain had left to be
sold to any chance traveller, or to towns-
people who might be inclined to purchase
them. There were several copies of Tate
and Brady's new Psalms, which some of the
New England Puritans wished to use instead
of the loved old Bay Psalm-book, two or
three Bibles, half a dozen volumes of ser-
mons, a Dutch Psalm-book, which was not
Dutch at all, but a collection of English
songs and ballads, Milton's "Paradise
Lost," a few prayer-books, and then there was
a wonderful book which Elam did not have
time to finish, though he had not wasted a
moment. It thrilled and filled him with
adventurous longings, and was called "Robinson Crusoe." This was the first and only
story-book he had ever seen, and as he retold
the wonderful tale to Cotton, the desire to
run away out into the great world, to cross
the ocean and see some strange sights and
lead a different life from that on a Narragansett farm, grew strong in both boys'
breasts.

At last Elam, having a fertile though unexercised imagination, developed a plan of action. They would leave home and meet at the old meeting-house, where they would spend several weeks of idleness, roaming the woods by day and sleeping in the noon-house by night, and when everyone in town was tired of searching for them, then they would make their way to the sea-shore without fear of capture, and get on board a ship and sail off somewhere. They could hide in the wood on the Sabbath days, and as the meeting-house stood on a lonely road in a great wood on the top of a high hill, there would be but few passers-by on week-days, and hence few chances of discovery. And now I must explain about the noon-house, which was to be their sleeping-place, for none of those queer old buildings now exist in New England.

By the side of the barn-like church were three long, low, mean, stable-like log build-ings, which could hardly be stables, since at one end of each hut was a rough stone chim-ney. These were noon-houses, or '' Sabba-day houses.''   One had been built by Elam and Cotton's grandfather, and was used by the families of his children.   Until the early years of this century, only two or three

meeting-houses throughout New England
contained stoves. All through the long,
bleak, winter weeks, through fierce " nor'-
westers " and piercing frosts, the lonely
churches stood, growing colder and colder,
until when they were opened upon the Sabbath the chill and damp seemed almost unbearable. The women brought to church
little iron foot-stoves filled with hot coals.
Upon these stoves they placed their feet, and
around them the shivering children sat at
their mothers' feet and warmed their chilled
hands. But by the time the long service
was over—for often the minister preached
two hours and prayed an hour, and some of
the Psalms took half an hour to sing—you
can easily see that the warmth would all
have died out of the little foot-stove, and
the mothers and children would be as cold as
the fathers, which is saying a great deal.

Now these half-frozen Baptists and Puritans and Episcopalians could hardly have
remained to attend an afternoon service and
lived through it, so they built houses with
chimneys and fireplaces near the church
where they could go and make a fire and
get warm and eat their lunch, and when
they asked permission to put up such a build-

ing they said it was to "keep their duds and horses in."

And, surely enough, at one end of the noon-house were usually several stalls for the horses, who doubtless also enjoyed the warmth that came from the fireplace at the end of the room. The "duds" were the saddles and pillions on which the church attendants had been seated on their ride to church, and the saddle-bags which were full of good things to eat. Sometimes a few cooking-utensils to warm the noonday food were kept in the noon-house, and often hay for the horses and a great load of logs to burn in the fireplace, and sometimes a barrel of "cyder," to drink at the nooning.

Frequently a large noon-house was built by several farmers in company, and I am afraid the children did not then enjoy their Sunday noontimes, for some old deacon or elder usually read a sermon to them between the morning and afternoon services, and they had to sit still and listen.

So you see that Elam and Cotton had very comfortable quarters to sleep in when they ran away to the noon-house on the Monday following the opening of my story. Each arrived about an hour before sunset,

laden with all the food that he had been
able to capture before leaving home. Cotton had a great piece of salt-pork and a
dozen eggs, some of which had had a rather
disastrous journey in his coat-pockets. Elam
had a great crushed mass of dough-nuts and
brown bread. This was not all of their
provisions for their sojourn, for on each suc-
cessive Sunday for five weeks previously both
boys had crowded their great pockets with
russet apples and their saddle-bags with cold
corn-bread and brown bread, and they had
starved themselves at each nooning in order
to save their food and thus provide for the
coming day of need ; and they had concealed
their treasures in an empty corn-bin at the
horses' end of the house. Cotton felt sure
that they had food enough to last them for
three weeks—rather dry and conglomerated,
to be sure, but still good enough for boys of
healthy appetites and simple Puritan tastes.
Elam also had brought a flint and tinder-
box with him, and with their aid and that
of some light " candle-wood " he soon had
a blazing fire upon the hearth, the coals of
which he carefully covered up to save till
morning, and then the two Robinson Crusoes climbed upon the hay and fell asleep.

The story of the first day spent by the
runaways in their retreat would be the story
of all the days, which were not as pleasure-
filled as they had hoped.   They had no hut
to build, no goats to tame, no savages to
fight and dread.   They rose early in the
morning, for the habits of their daily life
were strong, and they did not dare have a
fire much after daybreak, lest the smoke
from the chimney should be discovered by
some rare passer-by.   They ate their break-
fast of brown bread and cheese and apples
and drank a little of the hard cider.   As
the weather was fortunately warm, they
lolled on the stones behind the noon-house
while Elam told over and over again the
story of Robinson Crusoe and tales of the
Indians that he had heard from his grandfather.   They fished, with some success, in
a little brook which ran through the woods,
and one day they caught a rabbit in a trap
which Cotton had set, and which he had
learned how to make from old Showacum, a
" praying Indian " who lived in the village.
These trophies of their skill they of course
skinned and cleaned and cooked, and
though they were hungry—for they were
hungry all the time—the unsalted fish and

game did not seem very appetizing to them. They found a treasure one day in the woods —a store of nuts which had been forgotten or neglected or reserved until spring by some kindly squirrels—and with a few cakes of toothsome maple-sugar they had some variety of diet.

But alas, they also had healthy young appetites, and on Saturday night Cotton awakened to a fact whose approach had been plainly looming up before Elam for some time—that their three weeks' supply of food was all gone. A half-decayed apple was their sole supper. A drink of the sour cider seemed only to make their hunger harder to bear, but at last they fell asleep. Perhaps the pangs of his gnawing stomach made Elam sleep more lightly than on previous nights, perhaps the equally keen pangs of his awakened conscience may have made him restless, but at midnight he suddenly sprang to his feet with an exclamation of horror at a sound which he recognized at once as the howl of a wolf. He jumped to the fire, wakening Cotton, who tumbled out of his nest of hay with a bewildered and wretched expression and an impatient cry of, "Oh, why did you wake me up when I am so hungry ; pray let me sleep if you do or not," when nearer and louder still rose the mournful howl of the wolf. With trembling hand Cotton heaped the light wood on the blaze which Elam had started with the old leather bellows, and then threw log after log on the hearth until the blaze roared up the chimney. Of course, the wolves—for they could hear more than one—could not get into the noon-house, as window and shutter were fast, but the boys were so wretched with hunger, so homesick, so lonesome, that they hardly stopped to reason, and, trembling with fear, Cotton seized an iron "loggerhead" which his father kept in the noon-house, and thrust it into the coals to heat to a red-hot pitch, when it could be used as a weapon. A "loggerhead" was a bar of iron which was used as a stirring-stick in making "flip." Deacon Fayerweather always brought to church each winter Sunday in his saddle-bags three or four bottles of home-brewed beer and a bottle of Jamaica rum, from which, with the aid of the loggerhead, he made a famous jug of flip for the minister and deacons at the nooning.

And now the peaceful loggerhead was the only weapon the two wretched boys possessed, and, indeed, all they needed, for in a short time the howls of the wolves grew fainter and fainter and at last were no longer heard. All thought or power of sleep had, however, vanished from the brains of the, terrified young Crusoes at this experience of the pleasures of adventure. All wish for final escape to the sea-shore had also disappeared, and now their only longing was to return home. All the remaining hours of the night they sat by the fire, while Elam, romantic in spite of hunger, fright, and disappointment, made known his plans for the following day. Toward morning they let the fire die down and expire, and when the sun was fully risen they left their sheltering noon-house and hid in the woods not far from the meeting-house, trembling, however, at every sound as they thought of their dread night-visitors.

As nine o'clock drew near there approached the church on every side, on foot and on horseback, the members of the congregation. All knew of the mysterious disappearance of Cotton and Elam, for the country had been widely and quickly scoured for them. Among the worshippers came Deacon and Mistress Fayerweather and Goodman Noyes and his wife, for all felt it a godly duty, even in time of deep affliction, not to neglect the public worship of God on the Sabbath. Despairingly did the sad parents hope to hear some news of their lost boys, who had apparently vanished from the face of the earth, for neither in farm-house nor in field, neither on the road nor at the toll-gate, neither by traveller nor by hunter, had they been seen. The very simplicity of their plan had been its safety. Forty years previously the whisper of kidnapping by the Indians would have added terror to the parents' grief, but those days were happily over.

After sad greetings had been exchanged and the minister had entered the pulpit, the congregation seated itself for its usual Sunday-morning service. The opening half-hour prayer was ended, the church attendants had let down their slamming pew-seats (for the seats in those old New England meeting-houses always turned up on hinges to allow the pew occupants to lean against the walls of the pew during the long prayer), the minister had read with trembling voice a note which had been sent to him, "desiring the prayers of the congregation for two families in great inconveniency and distress," when

a door on the leeward side of the church
slowly opened and two pale, dishevelled, and
most wretched-looking youngsters crept slowly and shamefacedly in. The habit of constant
self-repression and self-control, characteristic
of the times, was all-powerful, even in this
intense moment of crisis for the families of
Fayerweather and Noyes. The deacon flushed
scarlet, but did not move from his raised seat
in front of the congregation. A faint murmur
swept over the entire assembly at the appearance of Cotton and Elam, but was at once
repressed. The boys walked calmly on to
their accustomed seats on the gallery stairs,
under the supervision of the tithingman.
That zealous officer rapped sharply on the
head with his long staff two or three of the
occupants of one of the "boys' pews," who
had turned around and stared, and whispered
noisily at the appearance of the runaways.
The old minister, being slightly deaf, had
heard no ripple of commotion, and, not having glanced at the late comers, proceeded
to offer a pathetic prayer for the lost ones,
"whom God held in the hollow of his hand,"
a prayer that brought to Elam and Cotton a
realizing sense of their selfishness and wick-
edness, and which worked a lesson that in-

fluenced them through life. The parson then
gave out his text: "He will have charge
over thee concerning thee," and worked his
way on in his accustomed and somewhat monotonous fashion, though with many allusions
to the two wanderers, until at fourteenthly
came the long-deferred end.   Nor was there
any murmur of feeling heard (though the
mothers' eyes were filled with tears), when
Deacon Fayerweather, in a slightly trembling
voice, lined out the Psalm:

O give yee thanks unto the Lord
   because that good is hee,
Because his loving-kindness lasts
   in perpetuitee.

I'th' desart in a desart way
   they wandered: no towne finde
to dwell in.   Hungry and thirsty
   their Soul within them pinde.

Then did they to Jehovah cry
   when they were in distresse
Who did them set at liberty
   out of their anguishes.

In such a way as was most right
   he led them forth also
That to a citty which they might
   inhabit they might go.

I wish I could say that the boys' parents, being so glad to get the wanderers home, permitted them to go unpunished, but alas! early New Englanders believed firmly that "foolishness is bound up in the heart of a child," and never spared the rod; and, as "sloathefulnes" and disobedience to parents were specially abominated, such high-handed rebellion as this of Elam and Cotton could hardly be allowed to pass by without being made a public example. Then, too, unfortunately for the boys, the warmth of joy at recovering the lost ones had time through the two hours of sermon to cool down and change into indignation. So at the close of the service Deacon Fayerweather, after rather coldly greeting his son and nephew, asked the advice of the minister upon so important a subject, who gave as his opinion that the gravity of the offence, the necessity of the lesson to other youths in the congregation, and the conveniency of circumstances seemed to point out plainly, and was furthermore upheld by Scripture, that public chastisement should be given upon the spot, and that Elder Rogers was best fitted, both by age, dignity, and strength, to administer both rebuke and punishment. And with promptness and despatch and thoroughness the decree was carried out; both boys were " whipped with birchen rods " while standing upon the horse-block before the church.

But though the colonial fathers were stern and righteously disciplinarian, the colonial mothers were loving and tender, as are mothers everywhere and in all times, and Mistress Fayerweather and Mistress Noyes each bore off her weeping boy to the noon-house and filled his empty stomach well with doughnuts and pork and peas and pumpkin-bread, until, with comfort and plenty within, external woes and past terrors were forgotten.

THE DOCTOR'S PIE-PLATES

THE DOCTOR'S PIE-PLATES

MANY of my cherished china treasures, having no historical association and being of comparatively coarse ware, would be of little value on the shelves of a collector, and also of little interest to the general observer ; but they are endeared to me by the remembrance of the circumstances under which they were found, or by some story connected with their past owner or their past history.

I have a set of dark-blue Staffordshire plates, known as the "Doctor's Pie-plates," which are resplendent with an interest that does not come from their glorious color, rich as it is, nor from the wit of the humorous scenes they represent. The plates, named, respectively, "Dr. Syntax's Noble Hunting-party," "Dr. Syntax Upsets the Beehives," "Dr. Syntax Painting the Portrait of His Landlady," "Dr. Syntax Taking Possession of His Rectory," and "Dr. Syntax Star-gazing," are printed from a

set of pictures drawn by Thomas Rowlandson, one of the most celebrated designers of
humorous and amusing subjects of his day.
They were drawn and engraved to illustrate
a book published by William Combe, in
1812, called "Dr. Syntax's Tour in Search
of the Picturesque." A second tour, "In
Search of Consolation," appeared .in 1820.
This was also illustrated by Rowlandson. A
third tour, "In Search of a Wife," was
printed the following year. These books
had an immense and deserving popularity.
Not only did these blue Staffordshire plates
appear, copying the amusing designs from the
Dr. Syntax illustrations, but a whole set of
Derby figures were modelled—Dr. Syntax
Walking, In a Green-room, At York, At the
Bookseller's, Going to Bed, Tied to a Tree,
Scolding the Landlady, Playing the Violin,
Attacked by a Bull, Mounted on Horseback,
Crossing the Lake, Landing at Calais, etc.,
and also were sold in large numbers.

The "Doctor's Pie-plates" did not, however, receive their name on account of
the presence of the laughable figure of Dr.
Syntax in their design, but from a far different and more serious and deeply felt reason. They were once used as pie-plates;

or, rather, I should say more exactly and
truthfully, were used *once* as pie-plates, and
the story of that solitary pie-episode in their
history, with the succeeding results of their
one period of use in that capacity, will explain their fresh, unused condition, and
show why I prize them so highly, and reveal also the reason why I call them the
" Doctor's Pie-plates." The name has a deep
significance ; the pie-plates are captured trophies of past war, sad emblems of hopeless
rebellion, never-fading ceramic proofs and
emblems of the selfishness, the tyranny of
man.

In the latter part of the eighteenth century, an American gentleman married in
England an English lady of some wealth.
They brought to America with them in a
sailing-vessel, as part of the bride's wedding-
outfit, a gayly painted, richly mounted trav-
elling-coach.   In this great coach they rode
in grand style with four post-horses from
Boston to Albany, New York, and Philadel-
phia, and back to the little town in Narragansett, which was ever after their home.
In due time they died, and left to their only .
son, a physician, all their worldly goods,
including the old coach, and the far less de-

sirable inheritance of a high and stubborn temper, and a firm and deep-seated veneration for English customs, manners, traditions, and productions, which would be worthy an Anglomaniac of the present day. He, however, made one unfortunate and incomprehensible deviation from his Anglo-worship when he married an American wife. As years went on, the Doctor grew more and more overbearing and dictatorial, especially in his household (as some English husbands are also said to be), and in the matter of food and of cooking—those unfortunate hobbies of an ill-tempered man—he took, perhaps, the most violent stand. Never did any other wife have to hear so often the words, "as my mother used to cook it," and "they don't do it so in England," or have to listen so frequently to acrimonious expressions of dislike of American cooks and cooking. Pork and beans, "cracker johnny-cake," Indian-pudding, even the purely Dutch dough-nuts were banished from his board; for not only did he refuse to eat these New England dishes himself, but would not let his wife and daughters, either. He also became unjust enough bumptiously to denounce as "Amer-

ican " and " taboo " any food (no matter of
what nationality) which did not suit his
fancy or which chanced to disagree with
him.

On an unlucky day, having eaten too
greedily of mince-pie (for he had a fine English appetite), he passed his universal ban-
ishing dictum on that darling of New
England hearts and stomachs — *the pie.*
From thenceforth on feast-days only English
plum-pudding was served for dessert. To the
New England wife, accustomed to see at
least *four* kinds of pie offered to " company," if one made pretence even of being
truly hospitable and housewifely, the lonely
pudding was a great and almost unbearable
source of grief and mortification, and many
a struggle did she make (trying to imitate
her forefathers of old) against the English
yoke, but in vain ; pieless and barren for
years was her table. But reinforcing troops
at last came to her rescue ; for three daughters
were grown, and, brave and strong with
youth, they dared to rebel more openly and
recklessly than their browbeaten mother.

In 1830 all the Doctor's relatives, far and
near, were invited to eat " Thanksgiving
dinner " with him and his family ; for he

was hospitable enough, in his own fashion;
in all, thirty were to sit down at his
board. On the day before Thanksgiving,
mother, daughters, and "help" were all
busy at work from early morning in the great
pantry and kitchen, making careful preparation for the coming dinner, and brisk sounds
of chopping and pounding and mixing were
heard, and savory smells and spicy vapors
filled the house. Toward the close of the
day, when their work was nearly done, they
suddenly heard, to their terror, the sound of
the Doctor's cane (for he was badly crippled
with that typical English disease, the gout)
thump, thumping through the halls and
rooms to the kitchen, an apartment he seldom visited. With palpitating hearts but
firm countenances they stood in a hollow
square for strength, as does any determined
band, while he walked past them to the
"buttery," where were placed in military
rows twenty-six of those hated abominations,
pies—mince-pies, pumpkin and apple and
cranberry, and, the crowning dainty of all,
"Marlboro'" pies. Their only hope of
salvation was that in the dull, fading November light the tyrant might not discover the
forbidden pastry; and, indeed, he did not

appear to do so, for he merely glanced scowl-
ingly around, and, without speaking, hobbled
back to his office.   Once more they breathed
freely, and the eldest daughter said, cheerfully: " Now, girls, nothing can happen ; if
he had seen them we should have had to
give them away ; but he won't know anything about it now until they are brought
on the table with the pudding, and he will
be most through his bottle of port then—but
oh, what shall we do when the company
goes ? "

Poor souls! they slept for one night the
happy, unconscious sleep of the victorious,
the hospitable, and awoke on Thanksgiving
morn to find every pie vanished from the
pantry-shelf.   Every pie?   Yes, and every
pie-plate, too !—twenty-six of the new English blue-and-white stone-ware plates.   At
first they really believed, in their simplicity,
that a thief must have entered from outside
and stolen them; but why should the ma-
rauder take pies, and no other food?   Then,
too, there was not a foot-print on the light
snow which had fallen early in the evening.
No ; the Doctor must have stolen his wife's
pies!   But where could he have hidden the
pie-plates?   For weeks, yes, for years, they

searched in every nook and corner; through the hay in the barns, behind the logs of wood in the sheds, in old barrels and boxes in the cellar, in closets, in trunks, under the eaves in the attic; and they even peered out on the roof behind the peaks of the gable-windows, but no pie-plates could they find. The grim old Doctor kept his silence, until his daughters grew at last to think that some thief must have entered in spite of apparent impossibility.

Thirty-six years later, in 1866, the aged Doctor died, and went, doubtless, to an English paradise. His browbeaten wife had given up the struggle many years before. The daughters, now elderly women, with a long-concealed but unsubdued hatred born of years of tyrannical browbeating and oppression, at once made a triumphal holocaust of many of the cherished treasures of the British tyrant; and the first victim doomed to destruction was the old English coach in which their English grandmother had ridden in state through the country. This broken-down, moth-eaten, rat-nibbled, cobweb and dirt-filled relic had stood unused for fifty years—an abominable nuisance, an inconvenient obstruction, a hated eyesore, in the carriage-house connected with their dwelling. The Doctor had cherished it on account of its English birthplace; but now its fate was sealed. As the first heavy blow of the destroying iconoclastic axe struck the hated coach, a loud rattle as of falling crockery was heard, and the executioner paused. A careful investigation discovered an unknown compartment under the driver's seat -which had been constructed for the purpose of hiding despatch-boxes and, perhaps, the bride's jewel-cases—and in this hiding-place were twenty-six dirt-covered, dark-blue Staffordshire plates. A sudden light of comprehension and recognition came into the faces of the sisters—here were the long-lost pie-plates! The cantankerous old Doctor had craftily arisen in the night, hobbled out silently, in spite of his gout, thrown the carefully and daintily made Thanksgiving pies to the pigs, stealthily packed the plates in the old coach, watched maliciously the unsuccessful plate-search, kept silence throughout the despoiled Thanksgiving dinner and through nearly forty pieless years, and died triumphant.

Half of this treasure-trove, which the Doctor could hide, but, happily, could not

take with him, were the Dr. Syntax plates;
and from that half came my share. The
other plates were of well-known English
views—Payn's Hill, the City of Liverpool,
Blenheim Castle, Fulham Church-yard,
Windsor Castle—no American views were
on any of his crockery; no landing of Lafayette, no State plates, were ever allowed to
grace that rank old Tory's pantry.

Thus, one good, one noble result came
from this "ugly trick"—the hidden pie-
plates were all saved unscratched, unbroken,
for the Doctor's kinsfolk to-day, who, in
gratitude for his unintentional posthumous
favor, suitably reward him by telling the
story of his spiteful midnight theft whenever
we show the plates. And, moreover, we
wantonly and openly insulted and jeered at
his memory and his gastronomic laws by
formally and derisively naming the dark-blue
salvage from the coach the Doctor's Pie-
plates.

MY DELFT APOTHECARY JARS

MY DELFT APOTHECARY JARS

THE circumstances under which I first saw my old Delft apothecary jars were so painful, so mortifying, that for a long time I could not bear even to think of them; but now, as years have passed and softened the sharp lines, I will write account of that unique adventure.

We were one day, as was our wont, hunting in old Narragansett for ancient china and colonial furniture, but even on that historic and early-settled ground had met with scant success. At last, on an out-of-the-way road, was found a clew.

We were driving slowly along, when the door of a long, low wood-shed opened, and an elderly man walked out on the single broad stone step and stood, in the lazy country fashion, staring openly and sociably at us as we passed by. He had in one hand a piece of dark wood which he was slowly rubbing with sand-paper. We had driven past his door when my companion suddenly exclaimed : " That man had a claw-foot."

" A claw-foot !" I answered in astonishment; " what do you mean ?—a cloven foot or a club-foot, perhaps ? "

" No, you goose; that man had in his hand a claw-foot—the leg of a chair, I am sure, and I am going back to see to what it belongs."

So we whisked the pony around and drove to the door where the claw-footed man still stood, and we then saw in the one dingy window a small sign bearing the words

ELAM CHADSEY
GENERAL REPAIRER

" Are you Mr. Chadsey ? " my fellow china-hunter asked. " We saw you with something that looked old-fashioned in your hand, and we thought you might have or know of some antique furniture or old crockery that the owners would be willing to sell."

" Wal, I ain't got any to sell ; I only mend furnitoor. I've got a couple of tall clocks in here repairin', but they ain't mine, so I

can't sell 'em. N–o—I don't know of none
—except— What furnitoor do you want?"

"Oh, anything, almost, that is old, and
china especially; any old blue pie-plates or
such things."

Elam stood slowly rubbing his claw-foot
and at last answered: "I know some old
blue-and-white crockery preserve-jars, or
jell-pots, ye might call 'em, which I ruther
think ye could get ef ye want 'em. Ye
see, Abiel Hartshorn, he's a widower an' he's
a-goin' ter marry a school-marm up ter Col-
lation Corners, an' she's got awful highty-
tighty notions, an' he's a-goin' ter sell the
farm, an' she come down ter see what things
she wanted saved out of the house fur her.
An' Abiel's fust wife she had all these old
blue-an'-white pots with letters on 'em, an'
some had long spouts, an' she always kep'
her preserves an' jelly an' sweet pickles in
'em, an' mighty handy they was too. An'
when this woman see 'em she was real
pleased with 'em, but her brother was along
with her, and he's a clerk in a drug-store,
an' he bust out a-larfin', an' says he:
'Them letters on them jell-pots means sen-
na, an' jalap, an' calomel, an' sweet syrup
of buckthorn, an' lixypro, an' lixylutis, an' all

sorts of bad-tastin' medicines.' An' then she fired right up, an' says she : 'I won't have any of *my* preserves kep' in them horrid-tastin' old medicine-bottles ;' so I guess Abiel would be glad enough ter sell 'em fur most anything.''

We suspected at once that these ''jell-pots '' with blue lettering of the names of drugs were Delft apothecary jars, and that the '' ones with spouts '' were the old jars, so rarely seen, that are identical in shape with the '' siroop-pots '' of Dutch museums. When the Dutch used these jars a century or more ago, they covered the open top with tightly tied oilskin and poured the contents from the spout, which at other times was kept carefully corked. By what strange, roundabout journey had these Delft jars strayed to that New England farm? We asked eagerly where we could see the de-spised ''jell-pots.''

'' Abiel's house is about two mile from here by the road. I tell ye what ye can do. Ye may as well see 'em now's ever. I'll walk cross-lots an' you drive there. Go on down the road a piece an' turn the fust road ter the right. 'Tain't much of a road—it's kind of a lane. Go on to the fust house ye come to. I'd better come, 'cause mebbe Abiel wouldn't let ye see 'em ef ye went alone.''

We left him and drove on and down through the narrow, grass-grown lane. When we reached the old gray farm-house we found it deserted and still, so we sat down on the stone doorstep and waited for Elam Chadsey, and soon he climbed over the stone wall before us.

"Ain't Abiel at hum? All the better! We'll go in 'n' see the preserve-jars, an' then he won't know any city folks want 'em an' won't put the price up on ye.''

He prowled around the house, trying in vain to open first the doors and then the windows, but to his amazement he found all carefully locked.

"The ninny !'' he said, indignantly, " he ain't got nothin' to steal! What did he lock up fur? I never heard of such a thing —lockin' up in the daytime; it makes me mad. The dresser stan's right in that room and them jars is on top of it; ef ye could only see in that window ye could look right at it, then ye'd know whether ye wanted 'em or not.''

"Isn't there anything I could climb up on?'' doubtfully I asked.

He searched in the wood-shed for a ladder, but with no success. At last he called out: " I guess ef you two'll help me a little we can pull this around fur ye to stand on."

" This " was a hen-coop or hen-house, evidently in present use as a hen-habitation. Its sides were about four feet high, and from them ran up a pointed roof, the highest peak of which was about five feet and a half from the ground.

" There," he exclaimed, triumphantly, as he pushed it under the window, " ef ye can git up an' stan' on that ye can see in. Then "—vindictively—" we'll leave it here fur Abiel to drag back himself, to pay him fur bein' such a gump as to lock his doors. I guess it'll hold ye, ef ye are pretty hefty."

I may as well state the annoying fact that to be " pretty hefty " is a great drawback in searches after " antiques." You cannot climb up narrow, steep ladders and through square holes into treasure-holding attic-lofts, as may a slender antique-hunter. You must remain patiently below and let her shout down, telling and describing what is above. It is such a trial to an explorer to have to explore by proxy, especially when you know you could discover more than anyone else

could. I determined that "heft" should
be no obstacle to me in this case, though the
hen-house did look rather steep and high ;
and I bravely started to climb. I placed
one knee, then the other, and then my feet
upon the ledge at the edge of the roof, while
Elam Chadsey pushed. He weighed about
one hundred pounds, and was thin, wizened,
and wrinkled to the last New England de-
gree. He braced his feet firmly in the
ground, set his teeth, and pushed with might
and main. Alone I scaled the second height.
I had barely set my feet firmly on the peak
of the roof, had shaded my eyes from the
sunlight with one hand, while I clung to the
window-frame with the other, had caught
one glimpse of a row of blue-and-white
apothecary jars, when — crack ! — smash !
went the frail roof under my feet, and down
I went—down into the hen-house !

In spite of my distress of mind and my discomfort of body, one impression overwhelmed
all others—the anguish and consternation of
Elam Chadsey. He darted from side to
side, exactly like a distracted hen ; he literally groaned aloud.

"Darn that gump of an Abiel Hartshorn !
He's the biggest fool in Rhode Island—

lockin' up his house jest 'cause he's goin'
away, an' gettin' us in this fix. Wait, miss,
keep still, an' I'll see if I can find an axe to
chop ye out.''

Wait! keep still!—indeed I would—I
couldn't do otherwise. Off he ran to the
wood-shed, and soon came back madder
than ever ; he fairly sizzled.

"Oh, the ninny! the big donkey! his
axe is in the house. What do you s'pose he
locked it up fur? He's a reg'lar wood-
chuck! I'll tell him what I think on him.
Ye ain't hurted much, be ye, miss?''

"Oh, no,'' I answered, calmly, "I'm all
right as long as I keep still. But if I try to
move there are several big and very sharp
splinters that stick into me, and nails, too,
I think—rusty nails, without doubt, which
will probably give me the lock-jaw. Oh,
Mr. Chadsey, do you suppose there are
many eggs in this house?''

"Not many hull ones, I'll bet. Oh, no ''
—very scornfully—"I s'pose Abiel took 'em
into the house to lock 'em up—the ninny.
He's the biggest ninny I ever see. Do ye
think, miss, if we could manage to tip the
hen-house over, that we could drag you
out?''

"No," I answered, vehemently, "the splinters are all pointing downward, and if you try to pull me out they will all stick into me worse than they do now. I have got to be chopped out of this trap, and you must go home, or somewhere, or anywhere, and get an axe to do it. Take our horse, and drive there, and do be careful when you go around the corners, or the cart will upset—and do, oh, do hurry. You must both go, our pony is so queer and tricky, and Mr. Chadsey might have trouble with him. Now, don't object, nothing can happen to me in my fortress."

So, rather unwillingly, they drove off, Elam Chadsey muttering to himself, "that Abiel Hartshorn's the biggest ninny in Rhode Island."

I was alone in my hen-house. I was not at all uncomfortable—while I kept still—though I was " cabin'd, cribb'd, confin'd." The true china-hunting madness filled my brain as I thought of the row of fine blue-and-white apothecary jars which would soon be mine, and other thoughts were crowded out. The calm and quiet of the beautiful day also soothed and cheered me in spite of myself. The wind sighed musically through the great ancient pine-tree that stood near the house. Flickering rays of glowing sunlight shone down on my head through the feathery foliage of the locust-trees that filled the door-yard. A great field of blossoming buckwheat wafted fresh balm in little puffs of pure perfume. Bees hummed and buzzed around me, and a meadow-lark sung somewhere near, sung and sung as if summer were eternal. A flood of light and perfume and melody and warmth filled me with sensuous delight in spite of my awkward imprisonment, and I fairly laughed aloud, and frightened the hens and chickens that had come clucking round me in inquisitive wonder at the removal and invasion of their home.

But my ill-timed and absurd sense of being in a summer paradise did not last long, for I heard in a few minutes the loud clatter of wheels coming down the lane from the opposite direction to that which had been taken by the hurrying pair. Of course, I could not see, for I had fallen with my face toward the house, and I did not like to try to turn around—it inconvenienced the splinters so. The sound came nearer and nearer, and at last I managed to move my head enough to see a country horse and wagon

with two men.   Then I leaned my face on
my folded arms, and I hoped and prayed
that they might drive past.   But, to my horror, to my intense mortification, they turned
and came up the driveway and underneath
the shed of the Hartshorn house.

A great dog bounded around and stared
at me.   I heard around the corner the murmuring sounds of suppressed laughter and
eager questioning, of which one sentence
only came distinctly to my ears: "Queer
sort of hens you keep, Hartshorn;" and
then the two men came round the house.

I hardly know what I said ; I think it was
this: "If you are Mr. Hartshorn, I must
beg your pardon for my sudden, impertinent, and most unexpected intrusion on the
privacy of your—hen-house" (here we all
three burst out laughing), "and I must ask
if you will please get your axe and chop up
your own hen-house in order to get me out."

Never speak to me again of Yankee inquis-
itiveness! Without asking one question,
Hartshorn ran into the house, brought out
his hidden axe, and while the boards were
firmly held by the other man (who, alas!
was young and well-dressed, and who proved
to be the city purchaser of the farm), Abiel

carefully chopped and split. I heroically bore this undignified ordeal in silence, until at last I was released.

"Come into the house," said Abiel, with wonderful hospitality to so impertinent an intruder; "ye must· be a leetle tired of standin'; come in and sit down. Ye ain't hurt much, air ye?"

"Oh, no," I answered, "only some deep scratches; but let me explain to you"—and I did explain with much self-abasement how I came to be fixed in my absurd position.

In the meantime the distracted pair had obtained the axe and were on their way back to the scene of disaster. As soon as they were within a full view of the house my companion china-hunter burst forth: "Why, she is gone! Where can she be? Do you suppose she has fainted and sunk into the hen-house? No, I can see, it is empty; she has got out of it somehow." Then she jumped out of the cart, ran up the path and through the open door, and found me sitting calmly talking with the well-dressed young man.

From the kitchen we soon heard sounds of violent and vituperative altercation.

"Abiel Hartshorn, yer the biggest fool I

ever see. What did ye lock yer house up in the daytime fur?"

"To keep out jest such pryin' haddocks as you and them be."

"Ye ain't got nothin' in it, anyway."

"Then what did you and her want to peek in fur?"

"Such a rotten old hen-house I never see."

"'Tain't made as a platform fur to hold a woman of her size."

"She don't weigh much."

"She do, too. Ye ain't no judge of heft, Elam; ye don't weigh enough yerself."

"What did yer lock up yer axe fur?"

"Ef I'd a-knowed yer'd a-wanted it so bad, I'd a-perlitely left it out fur ye."

"Wal, I never heard of sech a thing as lockin' up a house in the daytime, and yer axe, too—how could ye be such a fool? Say, Abiel, she looked funny though, didn't she?"

All's well that ends well. Abiel, having sold the farm, was glad to sell the roofless hen-house for two dollars, and he eagerly gave me the drug-pots. The former antique was never claimed, and the blue-and-white jars proved for many months too painful and

too hateful a reminder to have in sight.
Now they stand on table and shelf—pretty
posy-holders, but severe and unceasing moni-
tors.   Their clear blue letters—"Succ: E,
Spin: C," and "U: Althæ," and "C: Ro-
sar: R," etc.—speak not to me of drugs
and syrups, of lohocks and electuaries; they
are abbreviations of various Biblical prov-
erbs such as "Every fool will be med-
dling," "He taketh the wise in their own
craftiness," "Boast not thyself of to-morrow,
for thou knowest not what a day may bring
forth," "Let him that thinketh he standeth
take heed lest he fall," etc.   And the little
ill-drawn blue cherubs that further decorate
the drug-pots seem always to wink and to
smirk maliciously at me, and to hold their
fat sides as though they were thinking of the
first time they peeped at me and jeered at
me out of the window of the gray old farm-
house as I stood entrapped in my meddle-
some folly in the sunlight under the beautiful locust-trees in old Narragansett.

I cannot tell a romantic story of a further
acquaintance with the good-looking young
man; I never saw him again, and I am sure
I never want to.   Still, I know, ah, too well
I know, that he often thinks of me.   On that

susceptible masculine heart I made an impression at first sight.   When he welcomes visitors to his country-home I know he often speaks of his first glimpse of the house—and of me.   'Tis pleasant to feel my memory will ever bring to one face a cheerful smile, and furnish a never-failing "good story"— nay, to three, for I know that Elam Chadsey and Abiel Hartshorn both keep my memory green ; that to them my mishap was "argument for a week, laughter for a month, and a good jest forever."

THE DANCING TURKEY

THE DANCING TURKEY

In the States Papers office in London is a
" propper ballad " entitled a " Sommons to
New England," which was written about
1680. It alluringly recites natural conditions in the colonies. One verse runs
thus :

" There flights of foules doe cloud the light,
Of turkies three score pound in weight
As bigg as ostridges. "

All the early travellers in America con-
firm the vast weight of these wild turkeys—
Josselyn said sixty pounds. The turkey has
not grown larger by domestication, the wild
birds are still finer and more beautiful than
the tame ones. All foreign epicures agree
that American turkeys are the best in the
world. In America we make fine distinc-
tions, even in American turkeys ; tastes dif-
fer with localities. In some northern States
no turkey is perfect unless stuffed with chest-
nuts—that is, as food. In Louisiana he is

gorged with pecan-nuts. In South Carolina raw rice is your only prime turkey-food. In Virginia wild persimmons give the turkey a tang that gilds refined gold. The President of the United States, whoever he may be, feasts every Thanksgiving Day on a Narragansett turkey fattened on Narragansett grasshoppers—and I approve the President's taste.

These Presidential turkeys, though great and fat, are not "as bigg as ostridges;" but a Narragansett turkey with whom I was acquainted—as Rosa Bonheur would say— fairly rivalled his ancestors of colonial days.

His name was Launcelot Gobbo ; he was born, or rather hatched, on a Narragansett farm. He was the joint property of Bill and Ralph Prime, two farmer's sons, fourteen and fifteen years of age, who, according to the good old fashion in the Prime family, were given each year some portion of the farm stock—a cosset lamb, a brood of chickens, a pig, a cote of pigeons—to rear and sell, or keep as their very own. This year their share of the farm-products was Launcelot Gobbo and his mate. His name was given him by the village school-teacher, a

young college student who chanced to come
frequently to call on the boy's sister, Mary
Prime. Gobbo was chosen as their handsel
because he was such a mammoth turkey-
chick, a nine-days'-old wonder ; and by
tender cherishing he had fulfilled the great
promise of his youth.

This great size had been aided by careful
feeding, on a composite diet, of Narragansett fashion, extended by Oriental suggestion.
His first food was such as all well-reared
Narragansett turkeys have, milk curdled with
rennet, by which the gasps and stomach-
ache so fatal to turkey infancy were avoided.
Then came the natural food-supply of grasshoppers and Rhode Island whole corn. The
Prime boys had few books to read ; among
them were several dry and colorless memoirs
of sainted missionaries to the East. There
was one nutritious kernel, however, in one
of these rustling husks of books ; it was an
account of the preparation of locusts as food,
the roasting, frying, and drying them for
grinding them into meal. Bill Prime was
an inventive genius, a true Yankee, ever
ready to take a hint ; moreover, he was animated by sincere affection for his pet, and
pride in his size ; and as he read the meagre

missionary accounts he conceived the notion
of supplying Gobbo with his dearly loved
grasshoppers after autumnal winds had
chilled and cleared the fields of vegetable
and insect life.

It was not as easy a task to catch and dry
these American grasshoppers as Oriental
locusts, but love laughs at limitations ; just
as Gobbo laughed when his daily dole of
grasshoppers was dealt out to him on chill
October and November mornings, with the
Tallman sweetings that formed his dessert.
" Laugh and grow fat " is the old saying ;
and as Gobbo laughed he also grew fat, and
he waxed taller and taller. Ralph thought
Gobbo weighed thirty pounds ; Bill set the
weight at least five pounds higher. As the
turkey was full and rich of feather he looked
to me twice as large as any other I had
ever seen ; really big enough to reach the
seventeenth-century standard of " three score
pound in weight."

But Gobbo had other claims to consider-
ation besides his size or his distinguished
name ; he was an accomplished turkey—a
trick-performer. Like Shakespeare's famous
Gobbo for whom he was named, he "used
his heels at his master's commands." When

Bill struck the ground near him with a stick
and called out "Dance, Gobbo, dance for
the ladies," and set up a shrill fife-like
whistle, Gobbo spread his great fan-like tail,
and nodded and bowed his head, and cir-
cled and hopped around in exact time with
the rapping of the stick, in the most pompous, ridiculous, mirth-provoking caricature
of a dance that ever was footed or clawed.
He posed before the whole town as a show-
bird.   Stolid Narragansett farmers and fish-
ermen for miles around came to see him,
and roared aloud at his dancing, which he
had to exhibit every day in the week.   Even
on Sunday, at the nooning, Bill proudly but
secretly led the neighbors' boys home to the
farm and behind the barn; though the deacon sternly frowned on a Sunday dance,
even by a turkey who had no soul to be
saved.

It was the second week of November; Gobbo was still growing and still dancing, when
one day a gayly painted vehicle with a smart
horse came dashing into town.   The wagon
had an enclosed box behind the chaise front.
It might be taken for a peddler's cart or a
patent-medicine coach, but it was neither;
it was the collecting-van of a Boston "an-

tique-man." Persuasive, smiling, flattering,
peering into every kitchen, cupboard, and
dresser, in every parlor closet, in every bed-
room and gabled attic, he gathered in his
lucrative autumnal harvest of brass andirons
and candlesticks, of old blue dishes and copper lustre pitchers, of harp-back chairs and
spinning-wheels. He débonnairly purchased
two pewter porringers, a sampler, and an old
mirror of Mrs. Prime, while he effusively
praised the farm and the cattle. And as he
partook of the apples and cider generously
set before him, he shouted with laughter at
Gobbo, who proudly danced for him again
and again. As the early twilight began to
lower, the "antique-man" called out a
cheerful good-night and drove away. Gobbo
also stalked off—and forever—from the
Prime door-yard, for in the morning he had
vanished from the farm as completely as if he
had evaporated.

How the boys stormed and mourned ! how
fiercely they descended on the "colored"
Johnsons, more than suspected in the past of
chicken-stealing ! how they hunted the
woods and meadows ! how they fretted and
fumed !—but to no avail. To check their
worry and anger, their mother sent them off

to Boston to spend Thanksgiving week with
their married sister.

With the sea-loving curiosity of all boys,
they haunted the wharves and lower portions
of the city, and on the day before Thanksgiving, as they wandered up from the docks
through a crowded and noisy street, they
joined a little group gathered around the
show-window of a "dime musee," for in the
window stood as a lure, a promise of treasures
and wonders within, an enormous turkey,
penned in a wire coop, drooping of feather,
and listlessly feeding.

"He isn't nearly as big as Gobbo," said
Bill, contemptuously. "Not much," answered Ralph; but even as they spoke there
gathered in their questioning brains, in their
eager eyes, a conviction which burst forth
from their lips: "It is Gobbo!"

Now they were Yankee boys, slow but
shrewd, and they knew every feather of the
wings, every fold of the comb and wattle
of their pet; but each paid his dime and
entered the museum to be sure. Past the
voluble showman, the wax figures, the
stuffed animals, they silently strolled to the
window. No one else stood near within
doors. "Dance, Gobbo, dance for the

ladies !'' cried Bill, excitedly, striking the floor with his cane, and his heart beat high. Oh! how the crowd outside on the street laughed as Gobbo spread his tail and danced '' most high and disposedly,'' as the French ambassador said of Queen Elizabeth in the gavotte.

A great printed card hung over Gobbo's pen ; he was to be raffled that very night. Made suspicious by fraud, the boys scarcely dared leave the hall even for food, but with the instinctive good sense of many of country birth, Bill interviewed a friendly policeman on the beat, and another policeman appeared at the raffling at eight o'clock and sat near the Prime boys on the front row of seats in the hall.

At the appointed hour a noisy but not disorderly crowd had gathered. The master of ceremonies removed the wire netting from around Gobbo, who was still feeding and still fattening. The showman entreated silence, and in a reasonable stillness began : '' Gentlemen, this magnificent turkey, the biggest ever known in the civilized world, the feathered monarch of the ornithological world, will— ''when a shrill whistle pierced the air, and '' Dance, Gobbo, dance for the

ladies ! " was roared out. The turkey reared
his long neck and head like a snake, and with
a piercing gobble literally flew from the platform to his friend Bill, with a force that
almost stunned the boy. The showman
advanced : " What does this mean ? " he
shouted. " Don't you touch him," screamed
Bill, and " Don't you touch him," confirmed
with emphasis the policeman, while Ralph
explained to the inquisitive and sympathiz-
ing 'longshoremen and sailors who crowded
around him, how the turkey had been lost
and found ; not without some bitter asper-
sions on the character of the antique-man.

An adjourned meeting was held at the
police-station the following morning, when
the Prime boys testified and Gobbo danced,
and a gay session it was in those dingy
rooms; and the showman with a sham good-
humor resigned his claims to what had
proved to him a very lucrative drawing-card.

There ought to be a romantic ending to
this tale of a lost love; but every turkey has
his day, and this was Gobbo's. He was too
big to keep in a city yard, and too big to
take home in the cars; thus did his great-
ness, as did Cardinal Wolsey's, prove his
destruction. Even his accomplishments

were a snare; for when it was known he could dance, his talent could not be hidden under a bushel in obscure country-life. He had ever been destined for a city market, and soon again he graced a window, this time of a great city poulterer; and on the eve of Thanksgiving he was again raffled— the second time, alas! with hanging wings, and plucked sides, and drooping head.

CUDDYMONK'S GHOST

CUDDYMONK'S GHOST

BLACK CUDDYMONK and his wife Rosann
were holding an animated discussion as
they sat before the fire in their cheerful
kitchen in old Narragansett. That is,
Cuddymonk was talking loudly and effusively, while Rosann said little, but said
it firmly; and in the end succeeded in having her own way, as such stubborn, talk-
less persons usually do, whether they be
black or white. Cuddy had had an offer
of employment for a month, and he was unwilling to accept the position and do the
work; but Rosann calmly overruled him and
he had to yield. It was not that the work
was hard, or that the pay was poor, but
simply that Cuddy was afraid, he was too
superstitious to dare to face the terrors that
the performance of his duties might bring
forth. And yet it seemed simple enough!
Old Dr. Greene had the rheumatism and
could not hold the reins to drive, and he

wanted to hire Cuddy to drive in his chaise with him when he went on his daily round of visits, and to care for the horse when he returned home. Cuddy would have loved to feed and rub down the horse, and drive through the sunny lanes and green woods, and sit in the sun while the Doctor visited and dosed and bled within doors. It would be like making a round of visits himself, for he was then "Black Gov'nor," and at every house in village or on farm he would find some friend or constituent to chat and gossip with. But alas! all the Doctor's visits were not made in the daytime, and Cuddy shrank from the thought of driving all over Narragansett in the night. He thus complained to Rosann: "I wouldn't care if it warn't for dem darminted grave-yards. Dere's a graveyard on ebery farm all ober dis country. I nebber see sech fools es folks is in Narragansett. Dey warnts ter hab ghosts ebberywhere. Why don't dey keep 'em all in de ole church-yard ober ter Pender Zeke's corner, den yer can go de road dat leads round de udder way, an' not meet 'em. Down Boston way dey buries folks in church-yards an' keeps der ghosts where dey belongs."

Cuddymonk had travelled, and knew how things should be; he had ridden to Boston thirty years previously with Judge Potter; and the strange sights he had seen, and the new ways he had learned at that metropolis, had been his chief stock-in-trade ever since, and, indeed, had formed one of his great qualifications for election as Black Governor.

Rosann answered him calmly and coldly : "I's sick er ghosts, Cuddymonk. I'se been mar'd forty year, and you's a-talkin' about ghosts all de whole during time an' a-speerin' for ghosts all dem years, an' yer ain't nebber seed one yit. You's jess got ter go ter de Doctor's termorrer an' dribe for him."

"Rosann, when yer sees me brung home a ragin' luniac wid misery ob de head, yer'll wish yer hadn' drove yer ole man erway from yer bed 'n' b'ord ter go foolin' all ober de country in de night-time, seein' ghosts and sperits an' witches. P'raps I sha'n't nebber come home alibe, anyway."

"You's got ter go, Cuddy, an' dar ain't no use er talkin' 'bout it. I guess de ole Doctor kin charm off any ghost you'll eber see. 'Sides, he won't be out much nights when he got de rheumatiz ser bad. 'Tain't

ebry day yer kin git yer keep an' ten dollars
a month, an' yer ought ter dribe fer him
anyway, ter 'comerdate him, when he sabed
yer troo de bronchiters.''

So Cuddy went to the Doctor, and for a
week all was well with him. He drove to
all points from Wickford to Biscuit Town,
and received such greeting and honor from
all of his race as was due a governor. But
an end came to all this content, for late
on a misty, miserable September afternoon young Joe Champlin came riding up
to the doctor's door in great speed, and in
a few moments the Doctor shouted out to
Cuddy to harness up Peggy. Cuddy was
wretched. He knew well where the Champlin farm lay—far up on Boston Neck—and
he thought with keen terror of the lonely
road, of the many little enclosed graveyards
that lay between him and the Champlin
homestead. Fear made him bold, and he
managed to stammer out to the Doctor the
request that he would have Joe Champlin
hitch his saddle-horse behind the chaise and
drive the Doctor to the farm, where horse
and chaise and doctor could remain all night;
then he (Cuddy) would walk up early in the
morning to drive back. The Doctor scoffed

at the ridiculous proposition, and barely gave
Cuddy time ere they started to put on his
coat and waistcoat wrong side out—a sure
safeguard against ghosts. As they drove up
Boston Neck in the misty twilight Cuddy
suffered keen thrills of terror whenever he
got down from the chaise to let down bars
or open gates; for the only roads at that
time in that region of Narragansett were
drift-ways through the fields—well-travelled,
to be sure—but still kept closed by gates.
Cuddy clambered in and out of the chaise,
and opened and closed the gates with an
agility that amazed the Doctor, who had previously had frequent occasions in the daytime to revile him for his laziness in like
duties. He also glanced with apprehension
and dread at the family burying-grounds they
passed, counting to himself the whole dreary
number that would have to be repassed on
the way home.

These sad little resting-places are dotted
all over Narragansett. In olden times each
family was buried in some corner on the
family-farm. Sometimes the burying-place
was enclosed in a high stone wall; often they
were overgrown with great pine or hemlock
trees, or half-shaded with airy locust-trees.

Ugly little gravestones were clustered in these family resting-places—slate head-stones carved with winged cherub heads and quaint old names, and lists of the virtues of the lost ones; and all the simple but tender stone-script of the country stone-cutter's lore— hackneyed but loving verses—repeated on stone after stone. Beautifully ideal is the thought and reality of these old Narragansett planters and their wives and children resting in the ground they loved so dearly, and so faithfully worked for. But there was nothing beautiful in the thought to Cuddy; he groaned as he passed them, and thought of his midnight return; and he tried to learn from the Doctor how long he would probably be detained at the Champlin farm. But Dr. Greene, accustomed to ride alone for hours through the country, was taciturn and gruff, and kept Cuddy in ignorance of both the name and ailment of the patient.

When they reached the Champlin farm Cuddy ventured to say, with a cheerful assumption of interest: "'S'pose you'll stay here all night, Doctor, it's so cole an' damp an' so bad fer yer rheumatiz. I'll sleep in de hay in de barn an' won't bodder nobody."

"No, indeed," answered the Doctor,

sharply, " we'll start back in half an hour."
Cuddymonk gloomily hitched and blanketed
the horse, and walked into the great kitchen,
where, nodding and dozing, sat old Ruth
Champlin, the negro cook. When Ruth saw
his reversed clothing, she did not dream of
smiling at his absurd appearance, but at once
sympathized with him in his gloomy forebod-
ings ; and while she filled him with metheglin—a fermented mead made of water, honey,
and locust-beans—she also filled him with
fresh stories of witches and ghosts until the
time came to start on the homeward drive,
when the poor " Black Gov'nor's " nerves
were completely unstrung.

I will not give a list of the terrors that
assailed Cuddy from the first moment of his
ride home. A rustling leaf, a cracking branch,
a sighing wind, were magnified into groans
and wails. Every stone, every bush, seemed
an uncanny form ; every cluster of blackberry
bushes, every hay-rick, a looming monster.
And when Dr. Greene decided to return by
Pender Zeke's corner, and thus pass the old
church foundation of the Narragansett Church
and its cluster of deserted gravestones, Cuddy's
terror found words.

" Don' do it, Doctor ; don' go by dat dar-

minted ole church foundashum. It's a dreffle
lonely road, an' ebberybody knows dere's
ghosts in dat ole church-yard ebbery night.
Ole Mum Amey seed one a-dancin' on ole
Brenton's table-stone. Fer de lub ob praise,
Doctor, don' less go dere to-night. Ole
Tuggie Bannocks an' all dem dashted ole
witches gadders in de ole noon-house dat
stan's in de church-yard an' brews dere witch-
broth; an' ef anyone sees 'em a-brewin' dey
can nebber eat nothin' else, an' pines away
wid misery ob de stummick an' dies."

The Doctor only answered, gruffly, "Go
by the corners, Cuddy; I'll drive off the
ghost."

As they approached the haunted church-
yard Cuddy was fairly speechless with apprehension. His teeth chattered, and he held
the whip in one trembling hand to ward off
any ghostly or witchly attack. Words would
fail in attempting to express the horror, the
agony, which seized him, which overwhelmed
him when he saw as he passed the old noon-
house an unearthly, an appalling, object,
which he could not bear to look at, nor
could he force his staring eyes to look away
from. The Doctor saw it, too—a tall slender
column, about seven feet in height, of faintly

shimmering light vaguely outlining a robed figure, not of a human being, but plainly of a ghost. It appeared to be about a hundred feet from the road, though it could be clearly seen through the mist, and it seemed palpitating with a faint, uncanny radiance. "Stop, Cuddy," eagerly roared the Doctor, "I want to see what that is!" And as Cuddy showed no sign of stopping the horse's progress, he seized the reins from the negro's shaking hands. Cuddy, frightened out of all sense of respect or deference, shouted out, "G'lang, git up," and attempted to whip the steed.

"Cuddy, you black imp! if you dare to do that again, I'll whip you within an inch of your life. I'm going to get out and see what that is. It is a very interesting physical phenomenon."

"Oh, Doctor dear, you's bewitched a'ready. Dere ain't no physic about dat, it's a moonack. Fer de lub of God, don't go near it—you'll nebber walk out alibe"—and with that the unhappy black man fairly burst into tears and threw his restraining arms around the Doctor's neck.

The unheeding Doctor jumped from the side of the chaise with a force that nearly dragged Cuddymonk with him. The weeping negro's affection and interest would carry him no farther, and as the Doctor walked sturdily across the church-green, Cuddy, moaning and groaning in despair, gathered up the reins, ready, at any motion or sound of the ghost, to start the horse down the road and wholly desert the Doctor.

The brave ghost-investigator walked up the four narrow stone steps that once led to the church door—but now, alas ! lead sadly nowhere—then turned into the graveyard. As he stumbled eagerly along through the high grass and tangled blackberry-bushes, and as he passed under the shading branches of a wild-cherry tree, a most terrifying catastrophe took place—he plunged and slid into an open grave containing about a foot of water. Cuddy heard the splash, and it indicated to him the Doctor's utter annihilation. He gathered the reins up with a groan of despair and prepared to drive off with speed, lest the moonack chase and overwhelm him also, when he heard the Doctor's voice. The instinct of obedience was strong in him —for he had been born a slave—and he delayed a moment to listen. " Come here,

Cuddy," shouted the Doctor, "I've fallen
into the grave they've dug for old Tom Hazard." Cuddy groaned, but did not move,
either to drive, or to fly to the Doctor's rescue. " Come here, I say, and help me out ;
I shall die of the rheumatism if I stay here."
Another groan, but still no motion to render
assistance. " Cuddy, if you don't come,
I'll conjure you with that big skeleton in my
closet." Still no answer, and at last, the
Doctor, by dint of struggling and breaking
away the earth, managed to drag himself out
of the shallow grave. Undaunted by a mishap that would have both mentally unnerved
and physically exhausted anyone but a
country doctor, unchilled in spirit though
shivering in body, the determined inves-
tigator walked up to the ghost.

He took one glance and at once turned,
and, avoiding the open grave, ran down the
steps and across the green. " Come here,
Cuddy ; if I die of rheumatism I'll take you
up and show you that ghost. I'll conjure
you with every charm in the witch-book if
you don't come." Cuddy was weak with
terror, and the Doctor seized him by the
collar, pulled him out of the chaise and up
the steps. With chattering teeth and closed

eyes he stumbled along by the Doctor's side, clutching his leader's arm and muttering words of Voodoo charms. When they reached the faintly shining ghost, the Doctor shouted, "Open your eyes, Cuddy," and his power fairly forced Cuddy to comply. The Doctor raised his whip and brought it down on the shining ghost; a great swarm of fire-flies rose in the air, leaving disclosed a juniper-tree, which had chanced to grow somewhat in the form of a human figure. This strange phenomenon I cannot explain, but it is not the only time that a juniper-tree on a misty night in fall has attracted a swarm of fire-flies to light upon it.

Cuddy nearly fainted in revulsion of feeling. Both returned to the road and clambered into the chaise. The Doctor was now thoroughly chilled. He took from the medicine-chest that he always carried ("the Doctor's bag o' tools," Cuddy called it) a flask that may have contained medicine, but which smelled more like "kill-devil," and bade Cuddy drive with speed to Zeke Gardiner's; for when the heat of the chase was over, the valiant old Doctor began to feel the twinges of an enemy that he dreaded more than any ghost—his rheumatism—and he dare not ride home dripping with icy grave-water, even if he were full of Jamaica rum.

No lights were seen at Zeke's, but a vigorous knocking at the door roused the entire amazed and sympathetic family; and while one blew up a roaring fire in the chimney, another heated a warming-pan, another took off the Doctor's muddy clothes, and Mistress Gardiner concocted a terrible mixture—a compound tea of boneset, snakeroot, and chamomile, which, in spite of the Doctor's fierce remonstrances and entreaties for a mug of flip instead, she poured down his throat, thus cancelling in one fell dose many a debt of nauseous bolus, pill, or draught that she owed to him.

The perspiring Doctor, as he was being smothered in the great feather-bed, and singed with the warming-pan, and filled to the teeth with scalding herb-tea, gave his parting order to Cuddy—to drive home and tell Mrs. Greene that he had been detained at the Gardiners' all night " on account of an overdose of spirits," and then to come for him in the morning. Cuddy listened respectfully and answered obediently, went quietly around behind the Gardiners' house, calmly placed the horse in the Gardiners' stable and the chaise in the Gardiners' barn, slept the sleep of the brave, the obedient, the unhaunted, in the hay in the upper hay-mow, and appeared, as ordered, with horse and chaise at the front door the following morning.

www.ingramcontent.com/pod-product-compliance
Lightning Source LLC
Chambersburg PA
CBHW030828270326
41928CB00007B/956